Ignite

Michael Smith

Published by Michael Smith, 2024.

While every precaution has been taken in the preparation of this book, the publisher assumes no responsibility for errors or omissions, or for damages resulting from the use of the information contained herein.

IGNITE

First edition. April 4, 2024.

Copyright © 2024 Michael Smith.

ISBN: 979-8223687313

Written by Michael Smith.

IGNITED

Extraordinary Lives Shaping the 21st Century
The Spark Within: A World Transformed

Imagine the world you knew just twenty years ago. The internet was a novelty, smartphones were science fiction, and social media platforms were in their infancy. The landscape of science, communication, and social interaction has undergone a remarkable transformation in a relatively short period. This rapid advancement isn't a product of mere happenstance; it's the legacy of extraordinary individuals – the ignited minds who dared to dream beyond limitations and pushed the boundaries of what seemed possible.

This book is a tribute to these champions of the 21st century. We'll delve into the stories of pioneers in science and technology who have revolutionized the way we live, work, and connect. We'll meet fearless activists who fight for social justice and equality, their voices igniting movements that ripple across the globe. We'll encounter artistic visionaries who redefine the boundaries of creative expression, leaving an indelible mark on our cultural landscape.

These are not just stories of success; they are journeys fraught with challenges, setbacks, and moments of doubt. But within each champion burns an unyielding spark – a relentless pursuit of progress, a passion for making a difference, and an unwavering belief in a brighter future. Through their struggles and triumphs, they illuminate the power of human potential, reminding us that even the most audacious dreams can be ignited into reality.

The 21st century has been a whirlwind of change. From ground-breaking scientific discoveries to social movements that redefine the world around us, the way we live, work, and connect has been dramatically reshaped. But behind these advancements lie the stories of remarkable individuals – the ones who dared to dream, question, and challenge the status quo.

This book isn't just a chronicle of achievements; it's an exploration of the spark that ignites change. Within its pages, you'll encounter scientists pushing the boundaries of human knowledge, artists challenging societal norms, and entrepreneurs forging new paths. These individuals come from diverse backgrounds and disciplines, but they all share a common thread: the unwavering belief in the power of their ideas and the courage to pursue them.

As you delve into their stories, you might ask yourself: What ignites my spark? What change do I want to see in the world? This book isn't simply a collection of biographies; it's an invitation to discover your own potential and find your place in the ever-evolving narrative of the 21st century. Prepare to be inspired, challenged, and empowered. The future is being shaped right now, and your spark might just be the one that ignites the next wave of change.

Chapter 1: The Science and Tech Revolutionaries: Shaping Our World

The 21st century is undeniably marked by a surge in scientific and technological advancements – a renaissance unlike any other. This revolution has fundamentally reshaped how we live, work, and connect. It's a story not just of inventions and discoveries, but of the extraordinary minds who dared to push the boundaries of human potential.

These **science and tech revolutionaries** are the architects of our modern world. They are the ones who:

◇ **Questioned the status quo:** These pioneers weren't afraid to challenge long-held beliefs and established paradigms. They dared to ask "why?" and "what if?" in ways that led to ground-breaking discoveries.

◇ **Ignited innovative discoveries:** Their relentless curiosity and innovative thinking have led to breakthroughs across diverse fields. From gene editing to artificial intelligence, these revolutionaries are shaping the future.

◇ **Broke down barriers:** Science and technology thrive on collaboration. These revolutionaries don't just make discoveries, they inspire and empower others to build upon their work, fostering a global exchange of knowledge.

The impact of these revolutionaries goes beyond the lab or the tech company. Their work influences everything from medicine and communication to transportation and energy. They are creating a world with new possibilities and new challenges, and their stories serve as an inspiration for future generations to come.

This chapter explores the lives and achievements of such pioneers:

Dr. Jennifer Doudna
Decoding the Language of Life

Dr. Jennifer Doudna, a name synonymous with the revolutionary gene-editing technology CRISPR, has ignited a new era in biomedicine. Born in Washington D.C. and raised in Hawaii, her early fascination with science blossomed into a distinguished career in biochemistry. Her research delved into the complexities of RNA, a molecule long overshadowed by DNA but now recognized for its crucial role in cellular processes.

Dr. Doudna's pivotal moment arrived in a chance meeting with French microbiologist Emmanuelle Charpentier. Together, they unravelled the potential of a specific type of RNA – CRISPR – and its associated Cas9 protein. This discovery unveiled a powerful and precise gene-editing tool with the potential to rewrite the very code of life. CRISPR allows scientists to target and modify specific sections of DNA, offering unimaginable possibilities for treating genetic diseases, developing disease-resistant crops, and even altering human genes to eliminate inherited conditions.

Dr. Doudna's journey hasn't been without its challenges. The ethical implications of CRISPR gene editing have sparked fierce debate. Yet, her unwavering dedication to scientific exploration and responsible use of this technology continues to propel research forward. Dr. Doudna's story exemplifies the power of curiosity, collaboration, and a relentless pursuit of knowledge. She stands as a beacon of hope, igniting a future where genetic diseases may become a relic of the past.

Dr. Jennifer Doudna's name has become synonymous with a revolution in biology – the development of CRISPR, a revolutionary gene-editing technology with the potential to cure diseases, improve agriculture, and even rewrite the very code of life. This chapter delves deeper into her remarkable journey and the ground-breaking implications of CRISPR.

A Passion for Science Ignited Early

Born and raised in Hilo, Hawaii, Dr. Doudna's fascination with science blossomed at a young age. The natural wonders surrounding her instilled a deep curiosity about the world and how it worked. This curiosity led her to excel in science classes throughout her school years. She later attended Pomona College in California, where she majored in biochemistry, a field that perfectly combined her interest in biology and chemistry.

Delving into the Mysteries of RNA

After graduating from Pomona, Dr. Doudna's academic pursuits took her to Harvard University for her Ph.D. in biochemistry. While many researchers focused on DNA, the molecule long recognized as the blueprint of life, Dr. Doudna was drawn to the complexities of RNA (ribonucleic acid). Often overshadowed by DNA, RNA plays a crucial role in cellular processes, carrying genetic information and facilitating protein production. Dr. Doudna's pioneering research focused on understanding the structure and function of RNA, a decision that would prove pivotal in her future discoveries.

The Life-Changing Meeting and the Birth of CRISPR

A chance meeting in 2011 with French microbiologist Emmanuelle Charpentier marked a turning point in Dr. Doudna's career. Together, they delved into a specific type of RNA – CRISPR (Clustered Regularly Interspaced Short Palindromic Repeats) – and its associated Cas9 protein. Their research revealed that this system, used by bacteria to defend against viruses, had the potential to be repurposed for a revolutionary new tool: gene editing.

CRISPR acts like a pair of molecular scissors, allowing scientists to target and modify specific sections of DNA. This pioneering discovery opened a new frontier in biology, offering unimaginable possibilities for treating genetic diseases, developing disease-resistant crops, and even correcting harmful mutations in human embryos.

The Promise and Challenges of CRISPR

The potential applications of CRISPR are vast and transformative. Consider these possibilities:

- **Curing Genetic Diseases:** Scientists can potentially correct faulty genes that cause diseases like cystic fibrosis, sickle cell anemia, and Huntington's disease.
- **Revolutionizing Agriculture:** CRISPR can be used to create crops resistant to pests, diseases, and drought, leading to increased food security.
- **Gene Therapy:** This technology offers the potential to treat a wide range of diseases by altering genes directly within a patient's cells.

However, the immense power of CRISPR also presents ethical challenges. The ability to edit human genes raises concerns about designer babies, unintended consequences, and potential misuse. Dr. Doudna herself is a strong advocate for responsible use of CRISPR and actively participates in discussions about the ethical implications of this revolutionary technology.

A Beacon of Scientific Discovery

Dr. Jennifer Doudna's unwavering dedication to scientific exploration and her ground-breaking work with CRISPR have cemented her place as a leading figure in 21st-century biology. She is a testament to the power of curiosity, collaboration, and a relentless pursuit of knowledge. Her story serves as an inspiration for future generations of scientists to explore the mysteries of life and use their discoveries for the betterment of humanity.

Further Exploration: Delving deeper into the life and achievements of Dr. Jennifer Doudna.

Books:

- **A Crack in Creation by Jennifer Doudna and Samuel Sternberg:** This is Dr. Doudna's autobiography, co-written with science journalist Samuel Sternberg. It offers a first-hand account of her journey co-discovering CRISPR and the ethical considerations surrounding this powerful gene-editing technology.

- **He?—The Hunt for the Missing Piece of the Genetic Code by Siddhartha Mukherjee:** While not solely focused on Dr. Doudna, this Pulitzer Prize-winning book explores the history of genetics research, culminating in the discovery of CRISPR-Cas9. It provides context for Dr. Doudna's work and the significance of CRISPR in the scientific landscape.

Videos and Online Talks:

- **TED Talks:** Dr. Doudna has delivered several captivating TED Talks. Search for titles like "Editing the Human Genome" or "A New Era of Genetic Engineering." These talks offer a clear and engaging explanation of CRISPR technology and its potential applications.

- **Interviews:** Numerous online platforms feature interviews with Dr. Doudna. Look for interviews on platforms like PBS NewsHour, The New York Times, or scientific conferences. These interviews offer insights into her research process, her thoughts on the ethical implications of CRISPR, and her vision for the future of gene editing.

Check out an interview with Dr. Jennifer Doudna: https://www.youtube.com/watch?v=HANo__Z8K6s

Watch a video explaining CRISPR: https://www.youtube.com/watch?v=UKbrwPL3wXE

- **Documentaries:** Consider documentaries like "Engineering the Future" or "Human Nature Revisited" which explore the potential and challenges surrounding CRISPR technology. Dr. Doudna may be featured in some of these documentaries, providing her perspective on these issues.

Additional Resources:

- **The Doudna Lab Website:** The website of Dr. Doudna's lab at UC Berkeley (https://doudnalab.org/) offers information about her current research projects, publications, and the team members working alongside her.
- **Articles and News Stories:** Search for online articles and news stories featuring Dr. Doudna. Look for reputable publications focused on science, technology, and healthcare to gain insights into the latest developments in CRISPR research and the ongoing discussions about its ethical implications.

By exploring these resources, you can gain a deeper understanding of Dr. Jennifer Doudna's groundbreaking work, her motivations as a scientist, and the potential impact of CRISPR technology on the future of medicine and human health.

Stephen Hawking

A Life of Brilliance in the Face of Adversity

Stephen Hawking's story is one of exceptional intellect, unwavering determination, and a profound impact on our understanding of the cosmos. Here's a closer look at his remarkable journey:

Early Life and Education (1942-1963):

- Born in Oxford, England in 1942, Hawking displayed a natural curiosity for science from a young age.
- Despite his father's encouragement towards medicine, Hawking pursued physics at University College, Oxford, graduating with first-class honours in 1962.
- In 1963, at the age of 21, Hawking received a devastating diagnosis of amyotrophic lateral sclerosis (ALS), a progressive neurodegenerative disease that gradually paralyzes the body. Doctors gave him only a few years to live.

Defying the Odds: Research and Breakthroughs (1963-1980s):

- Refusing to be defined by his illness, Hawking continued his studies at Cambridge, obtaining his Ph.D. in applied mathematics and theoretical physics in 1966.
- He focused on general relativity and cosmology, exploring the nature of black holes and the origins of the universe.
- Hawking's ground-breaking work included:
    - **Black Hole Radiation (Hawking Radiation):** Proposed that black holes, contrary to their name, emit a form of radiation due to quantum effects near their event horizon.
    - **Singularities:** Contributed to the understanding of singularities, points of infinite density and gravity believed to

exist at the center of black holes and the beginning of the
universe.

- Despite his increasing physical limitations, Hawking's
  research flourished. He developed new methods of working,
  using a speech synthesizer after losing his ability to speak in
  the 1980s.

-

A Legacy of Knowledge and Inspiration (1980s-2018):

- In 1988, Hawking published his most famous book, "A Brief
  History of Time," which brought cosmology to a popular
  audience and became a worldwide bestseller.
- He continued to write extensively, making complex scientific
  ideas accessible to the public. Some of his other notable
  books include:
    - *The Grand Design* (2010) - Explores the nature of reality and
      the possibility of a unified theory of everything.
    - *Black Holes and Baby Universes and Other Essays* (1993) - A
      collection of essays on various topics in cosmology and physics.
- Hawking actively participated in scientific discussions and
  debates, advocating for further exploration of the universe.
- He received numerous accolades for his work, including the
  Order of the British Empire and the Presidential Medal of
  Freedom.

Beyond Science: A Life of Advocacy and Personal Triumphs:

- Hawking's life transcended scientific achievement. He was a
  strong advocate for people with disabilities and a champion
  of scientific literacy.
- He married twice and had three children, demonstrating a
  fulfilling personal life alongside his scientific pursuits.

Further Exploration:

- **Videos:**
  - My Brief History Stephen Hawking: YouTube: A documentary exploring Hawking's life and work.
  - Stephen Hawking - A Brief History Of Time [1] Our Picture Of The Universe[1]: Hawking himself delivers a lecture on the origins of the universe.
  - The Life of Stephen Hawking - Educational Video for Kids: YouTube: A kid-friendly introduction to Hawking's life and achievements.
- **Books:**
  - *A Brief History of Time* by Stephen Hawking
  - *My Brief History* by Stephen Hawking (his autobiography)

Stephen Hawking's story is an inspiration for anyone facing adversity. His unwavering dedication to science, his ability to communicate complex ideas, and his resilience in the face of illness all leave a lasting legacy. He opened doors to a deeper understanding of the universe and continues to inspire generations of scientists and science enthusiasts.

---

1. https://gemini.google.com/app/YouTube

Lise Meitner

A Pioneering Physicist Overshadowed by History

Lise Meitner's story is one of ground-breaking scientific contributions, resilience in the face of prejudice, and an unwavering passion for understanding the universe. Despite her fundamental role in the discovery of nuclear fission, recognition for her work was often overshadowed by circumstance.

Early Life and Education (1878-1906):

- Born in Vienna, Austria in 1878, Lise Meitner belonged to an assimilated Jewish family. Though girls weren't typically afforded higher education, Lise's father ensured she received private tutoring, fostering her love for mathematics and science.
- Defying societal norms, Meitner entered the University of Vienna in 1901, becoming only the second woman to earn a doctorate in physics in 1906.

A Pioneering Partnership (1907-1938):

- Unable to secure an official academic position due to her gender, Meitner moved to Berlin in 1907. There, she met Otto Hahn, a chemist, and the two embarked on a highly successful research collaboration that would span over three decades.
- Together, they made significant discoveries in the field of radioactivity, including the element protactinium in 1917.
- Meitner's expertise in physics complemented Hahn's skills in chemistry, making them a formidable team.

Nuclear Fission and Forced Escape (1938-1939):

- With the rise of Nazi Germany, Meitner, being Jewish, faced increasing persecution. In 1938, she was forced to flee Austria and seek refuge in Sweden.
- Despite the separation, Meitner continued collaborating with Hahn through letters.
- In late 1938, they conducted theoretical work that led to the explanation of nuclear fission, a process where a heavy nucleus splits into lighter nuclei, releasing a tremendous amount of energy. This discovery laid the groundwork for the development of nuclear power and nuclear weapons.
- Unfortunately, due to Meitner's exile and the political climate, Hahn received sole credit for the discovery in the published paper.

Later Life and Recognition (1939-1968):

- While she never received the Nobel Prize for her work on nuclear fission, Meitner continued her research in Sweden, making significant contributions to nuclear physics.
- Over time, her role in the discovery of nuclear fission became more widely recognized.
- In 1967, the element Meitnerium (Mt) was named in her honour, a testament to her lasting legacy.

Lise Meitner's Legacy:

- Lise Meitner's story is a powerful reminder of the contributions women have made to science, often overcoming significant obstacles.
- Her ground-breaking research in radioactivity and her role in deciphering nuclear fission continue to hold immense

importance in our understanding of the universe and the potential of nuclear energy.

- Beyond her scientific achievements, Meitner serves as an inspiration for her unwavering dedication to knowledge and her resilience in the face of adversity.

Delving Deeper into Lise Meitner's Remarkable Life

Lise Meitner's story is one that deserves to be explored further. Here are some resources to help you gain a deeper understanding of her remarkable journey:

Videos:

- **Lise Meitner's Discover of Nuclear Fission** (YouTube): https://www.youtube.com/watch?v=6UvbdidT-qM - A concise explanation of Meitner and Hahn's collaboration and the discovery of nuclear fission.
- **Panel: The Life and work of Lise Meitner** (YouTube): https://www.youtube.com/watch?v=uZZFG58G_jE - A panel discussion offering insights into Meitner's life and achievements.

Books:

- **Lise Meitner: A Life in Physics** by Ruth Lewin Sime: A comprehensive biography detailing Meitner's scientific contributions and personal struggles.
- **Fisgon Girl: Lise Meitner's Escape from Nazi Germany and Her Role in the Manhattan Project** by Melanie Wind Fine: Explores Meitner's escape from Nazi persecution and her indirect connection to the Manhattan Project.

- **The Woman Who Split the Atom: The Life of Lise Meitner** by Marissa Moss: A biography geared towards a younger audience, making it a great starting point to learn about Meitner's life.

Websites:

- **Atomic Archive: Lise Meitner** https://www.nytimes.com/2023/10/02/science/lise-meitner-fission-nobel.html: Provides a brief overview of Meitner's life and accomplishments.
- **AIP | The Niels Bohr Library & Archives: Lise Meitner Papers** https://www.aip.org/sites/default/files/history/files/newsletter-pdf/spring07.pdf: The American Institute of Physics offers access to a digital collection of Meitner's papers, allowing for a glimpse into her scientific work.

These resources provide a springboard for further exploration. You can delve deeper into specific aspects of Meitner's life and work, such as her research on radioactivity or the ethical considerations surrounding nuclear fission.

Lise Meitner's story reminds us of the importance of recognizing the contributions of women and marginalized groups in science. Her brilliance and dedication continue to inspire scientists and researchers today.

Tim Berners-Lee

Weaving the World Wide Web

Tim Berners-Lee is a visionary computer scientist credited with inventing the World Wide Web, the revolutionary technology that transformed how we access and share information. Here's a glimpse into his journey:

Early Life and Influences (1955-1980):

- Born in London in 1955, Berners-Lee's parents were both computer scientists who worked on the Ferranti Mark 1, one of the first commercial computers. This early exposure to technology sparked his lifelong interest in the field.
- He studied physics at Oxford University, where he built his own computer out of salvaged parts. This experience nurtured his problem-solving skills and passion for creating tools.
- After graduating in 1978, Berners-Lee worked as a software engineer for several years. During this time, he encountered the limitations of existing information sharing methods, which often involved complex, non-intuitive systems.

The Birth of the Web (1980-1990):

- In 1980, Berners-Lee joined the European Organization for Nuclear Research (CERN) in Switzerland. Here, the challenges of sharing information among scientists from various countries became particularly apparent.
- In 1989, Berners-Lee proposed a project called "WorldWideWeb" – a hypertext system that would allow users to access information through linked documents.

- He developed the fundamental technologies that power the web today, including:
    - **Hypertext Transfer Protocol (HTTP):** The communication language between web servers and browsers.
    - **Uniform Resource Identifier (URI):** A standardized system for addressing resources on the web.
    - **Hypertext Markup Language (HTML):** The code used to structure and format web pages.
- By 1990, Berners-Lee had built the first web browser and web server, demonstrating the functionality of his invention.

•

Championing Openness and Accessibility (1990-Present):

- Recognizing the web's potential to revolutionize communication globally, Berners-Lee refused to patent his creation. He believed it should remain open and accessible to all.
- In 1994, he founded the World Wide Web Consortium (W3C) to oversee the web's ongoing development and ensure its standards remain open and interoperable.
- Throughout his career, Berners-Lee has been a vocal advocate for a neutral and equitable web, expressing concerns about issues like net neutrality and online privacy.
- He continues to champion the web's potential to empower individuals and societies while working to address its challenges.

Tim Berners-Lee's Legacy:

- Tim Berners-Lee's invention transformed how we access information, connect with each other, and conduct business. The World Wide Web has become an indispensable tool for communication, education, and global collaboration.
- Beyond the technology itself, Berners-Lee's commitment to openness and accessibility has shaped the web into a platform for knowledge sharing and innovation. His vision continues to guide the web's evolution and its potential to shape our future.

Delving Deeper into Tim Berners-Lee's Web of Achievements

Tim Berners-Lee's creation, the World Wide Web, has fundamentally altered how we interact with the world. Here are some resources to explore his life and work further:

Videos:

- **Weaving the Web: The Original Design of the World Wide Web** (TED Talk): https://www.ted.com/talks/tim_berners_lee_the_next_web?language=en - Berners-Lee himself delivers a captivating talk on the origins and design principles of the web.
- **Revolution OS** (Documentary film): While not solely focused on Berners-Lee, this documentary explores the open-source software movement, a philosophy central to his vision for the web.

Books:

- **Weaving the Web: The Past, Present and Future of the World Wide Web by Tim Berners-Lee:** An autobiography by Berners-Lee himself, offering insights into his thought process, motivations, and concerns about the web's future.
- **The World Wide Web: A History by James Gillies and Richard Golding:** Provides a broader historical context for the web's development and its impact on society.

Websites:

- **World Wide Web Foundation:** https://webfoundation.org/

- Founded by Berners-Lee, this organization works to ensure a web that is open, safe, and empowers everyone.
- **W3C (World Wide Web Consortium):** https://www.w3.org/ - The organization Berners-Lee established to oversee the web's technical development and maintain its open standards.

Articles:

- **Long Now Foundation Interview with Tim Berners-Lee:** https://longnow.org/talks/ - An in-depth interview where Berners-Lee discusses his long-term vision for the web's role in society.

These resources provide a Launchpad for further exploration. You can delve deeper into specific aspects of Berners-Lee's work, such as the technical underpinnings of the web or his ongoing fight for net neutrality and online privacy.

Rosalyn Yalow

Pioneering Physicist Who Revolutionized Medical Diagnosis

Rosalyn Yalow's story is one of scientific brilliance, perseverance in the face of gender barriers, and a discovery that transformed medical diagnostics. Her development of radioimmunoassay (RIA) remains a cornerstone of modern medicine.

Early Life and Education (1921-1945):

- Born in New York City in 1921, Rosalyn Sussman displayed a natural curiosity for science from a young age. Despite her family's modest background, she excelled in school and pursued physics, a field uncommon for women at the time.

- After graduating from Hunter College in 1941, Yalow faced rejection from graduate physics programs due to her gender and religion (Jewish). Undeterred, she took a secretarial job at the University of Illinois and impressed a biochemist with her scientific knowledge. This led to her acceptance into the university's physics graduate program.
- In 1945, she married Aaron Yalow, a fellow physics student, and they embarked on a scientific partnership that would last throughout their careers.

A Pioneering Collaboration (1945-1970s):

- After earning her Ph.D. in nuclear physics in 1948, Yalow joined the Bronx Veterans Administration Hospital (VA) as a researcher. There, she began collaborating with Dr. Solomon Berson, a physician, to investigate the use of radioisotopes in medical research.
- Their initial focus was on understanding how the body regulates insulin levels in patients with diabetes. Existing methods for measuring insulin were cumbersome and inaccurate.
- Yalow and Berson's ground-breaking innovation came in the 1960s with the development of radioimmunoassay (RIA). This technique uses radioactive isotopes as tracers to measure minute amounts of hormones, proteins, and other substances in the blood. RIA revolutionized medical diagnostics by allowing for the accurate and sensitive detection of various diseases, including:
  - Diabetes, Thyroid disorders, Cancer and Fertility problems

Recognition and Legacy (1970s-2011):

- Yalow's ground-breaking work earned her numerous accolades. In 1977, she became the first American woman to receive the Nobel Prize in Physiology or Medicine, sharing the honour with Dr. Berson.
- Throughout her career, Yalow continued to refine and expand the applications of RIA. She actively advocated for women in science and mentored countless researchers.
- Rosalyn Yalow passed away in 2011, leaving behind a legacy that transformed the field of medicine. RIA remains a vital tool used in countless diagnostic tests today.

Yalow's story is more than a scientific achievement. It highlights the importance of perseverance in the face of barriers and the power of collaboration. Her legacy inspires future generations of scientists, particularly women, to pursue their dreams in science and medicine.

Delving Deeper into Rosalyn Yalow's Pioneering Legacy

Rosalyn Yalow's development of radioimmunoassay (RIA) stands as a landmark achievement in medical diagnostics. Here are some resources to explore her life and work further:

Videos:

- **Rosalyn Sussman Yalow - Nobel Laureate in Physiology or Medicine 1977** (National Institutes of Health): https://www.youtube.com/watch?v=Kk7ViRvJquM - An interview with Yalow herself, discussing her background, the development of RIA, and its impact on medicine.

Books:

- **Rosalyn Yalow: Nobel Laureate: Her Life and Work in Medicine** by Eugene Straus: A biography written by Yalow's long-time colleague, offering insights into her scientific journey, personal struggles, and unwavering dedication to research.
- **Breaking Barriers: The Inspiring Story of Rosalyn Yalow** by Teri Perl: Aimed at a younger audience, this book chronicles Yalow's life and accomplishments in a captivating and accessible way.
-

- **Websites:**

- **National Institutes of Health - Rosalyn Yalow Biography** https://www.nobelprize.org/prizes/medicine/1977/yalow/facts/: Provides a concise overview of Yalow's life and scientific contributions.
- **Jewish Women's Archive - Rosalyn Yalow** https://jwa.org/encyclopedia/content/Y: Explores Yalow's experiences as a Jewish woman in science and her impact on breaking down gender barriers.

Articles:

- **A Conversation with Rosalyn Yalow** (Scientific American): https://www.scientificamerican.com/issue/sa/2024/03-01/ - An in-depth interview where Yalow discusses her scientific approach, the importance of collaboration, and her views on the future of medicine.

These resources highlight Yalow's remarkable journey and the enduring impact of her work. You can delve deeper into specific aspects of her life and achievements, such as the technical details of RIA or her advocacy for women in science.

Rosalyn Yalow's story is an inspiration for anyone pursuing a career in science or medicine. Her unwavering dedication, scientific brilliance, and commitment to breaking barriers continue to inspire future generations of researchers and healthcare professionals.

Elon Musk

Architect of a Multi-planetary Future

Few figures embody the audacity and disruptive spirit of 21st-century technology like Elon Musk. Born in Pretoria, South Africa, his entrepreneurial spark ignited early, leading him to co-found companies like X.com (later becoming PayPal) that revolutionized online finance. But Musk's ambitions extend far beyond the realm of digital transactions. His vision is set on a future where humanity transcends the limitations of Earth, venturing into the cosmos and ensuring the long-term survival of our species.

This vision fuels two of Musk's most audacious ventures: SpaceX and Tesla. SpaceX, founded in 2002, aims to slash the cost of space travel and make humanity a multi-planetary species. By developing reusable rockets like the Falcon 9 and the Starship SpaceX has challenged the status quo in the aerospace industry and opened doors for more affordable space exploration.

Tesla, launched in 2003, is at the forefront of the electric vehicle revolution. Musk's vision is for a sustainable future powered by clean energy, and Tesla's sleek electric cars and innovative battery technology are paving the way. Beyond automobiles, Tesla is disrupting the energy sector with its Power wall home battery systems, promoting energy independence and a shift towards renewable sources.

Musk's ventures haven't been without their share of challenges. Technical setbacks, production delays, and ambitious timelines have garnered both praise and criticism. However, his unwavering belief in his vision and relentless pursuit of innovation continue to propel him forward. Elon Musk stands as a testament to the power of audacious dreams and the potential for technological advancements to reshape our world. He is a true "science and tech revolutionary," igniting a path towards a future where humanity reaches for the stars and embraces a sustainable future on Earth.

Elon Musk: A Visionary Architect of the Future

Elon Musk, the name synonymous with electric cars, space exploration, and audacious dreams, is a true 21st-century visionary. This chapter delves into the life of this remarkable entrepreneur and the ways his companies, Tesla, SpaceX, and Neuralink, are revolutionizing various industries and pushing the boundaries of human potential.

From Pretoria to Silicon Valley: A Life Fuelled by Innovation

Born in Pretoria, South Africa in 1971, Elon Musk displayed an aptitude for technology and invention from a young age. He wrote and sold his first computer program at the age of 12 and later moved to Canada to pursue his educational ambitions. After completing his bachelor's degrees in physics and economics at the University of Pennsylvania, he embarked on graduate studies in physics at Stanford University. However, the burgeoning dot-com boom ignited his entrepreneurial spirit, leading him to leave Stanford after just two days to pursue his first business venture, Zip2, an online city guide software company.

Building a Silicon Valley Empire: PayPal, Tesla, and SpaceX

Zip2's success served as a springboard for Musk's next venture, X.com, an online financial services company that later merged with Confinity, a company specializing in money transfers. This merger formed PayPal, a revolutionary online payment platform that would be acquired by eBay for a staggering $1.5 billion in 2002. This early financial success allowed Musk to set his sights on even more ambitious goals: revolutionizing transportation and colonizing Mars.

In 2002, Musk invested in and became CEO of a fledgling electric car company called Tesla Motors. At the time, electric vehicles were seen as a niche market with limited potential. However, Musk envisioned a future powered by sustainable energy and believed electric cars could be both stylish and powerful. Tesla's journey wasn't without its challenges, but under Musk's leadership, the company has become a global leader in electric vehicle technology, with iconic models like the Model S and Model 3 leading the charge.

Beyond electric cars, Musk set his sights on space exploration with the founding of SpaceX in 2002. His goal: to make space travel more affordable and accessible, ultimately enabling the colonization of Mars. SpaceX has revolutionized the aerospace industry by developing reusable rockets, dramatically reducing launch costs and paving the way for a more sustainable future in space exploration. The company's successful missions, including delivering cargo to the International Space Station and launching NASA astronauts into orbit, have solidified SpaceX's position as a major player in the new space race.

Beyond Electric Cars and Rockets: Neuralink and the Future of Brain-Computer Interfaces

Never one to shy away from bold ideas, Musk co-founded Neuralink in 2016. This neurotechnology company aims to develop brain-computer interfaces (BCIs) that could revolutionize our interaction with technology and potentially even enhance human capabilities. While still in its early stages, Neuralink's research holds immense promise for the treatment of neurological disorders, control of prosthetic limbs, and even the potential to augment human cognition.

A Visionary with a Relentless Drive

Elon Musk is a controversial figure, known for his ambitious pronouncements, workaholic tendencies, and occasional social media gaffes. However, his unwavering dedication to innovation and his ability to inspire others are undeniable. His companies, Tesla, SpaceX, and Neuralink, are pushing the boundaries of what's possible in transportation, space exploration, and brain-computer interfaces. Whether colonizing Mars or merging human and machine intelligence, Musk's vision for the future is as audacious as it is inspiring.

Dive Deeper into Elon Musk's World: A Journey Beyond the Headlines

Elon Musk, the visionary entrepreneur behind Tesla, SpaceX, and other audacious ventures, has captivated the world with his ambition and drive to revolutionize various industries. Here are some resources to delve deeper into his life, achievements, and the ideas that fuel his relentless pursuit of innovation:

Books:

- **Elon Musk: Tesla, SpaceX, and the Quest for a Fantastic Future by Ashlee Vance:** This detailed biography by Ashlee Vance offers a comprehensive look at Musk's life, from his childhood to his rise to tech superstardom. It explores his motivations, the challenges faced by his companies, and his vision for the future.
- **Elon Musk: Inventing the Future by Vance, Ashlee [2021] (Audiobook):** An audiobook version of Vance's biography allows you to learn about Musk on the go.
- **Liftoff: How SpaceX Took Center Stage in the New Space Race by Eric Berger:** This book delves specifically into SpaceX, detailing the company's history, its ambitious goals of colonizing Mars, and the challenges it faces in achieving them.
- **Playing with Fire: How SpaceX Gambled Everything to Revolutionize Silicon Valley by Leslie Hook:** This book offers a behind-the-scenes look at the early days of SpaceX, highlighting the risks, setbacks, and triumphs that shaped the company.
- **Read an article** about Neuralink: https://neuralink.com/

Videos and Online Talks:

- **TED Talks:** While Elon Musk himself hasn't delivered a TED Talk, there are TED Talks featuring interviews with him or discussing his work. Look for titles like "Elon Musk: The future we're building - and why it matters" or "How Elon Musk is changing the world."

Watch a talk by Elon Musk: https://www.ted.com/speakers/elon_musk

- **Interviews and Conferences:** Numerous online platforms feature interviews with Musk. Search for platforms like 60 Minutes, Lex Fridman Podcast, or conferences focused on technology, space exploration, or artificial intelligence.
- **Company Live streams:** Both Tesla and SpaceX occasionally host live stream events where Musk discusses company updates, upcoming projects, and his vision for the future. Check the companies' websites or social media channels for upcoming events.
- **Documentaries:** Documentaries like "Elon Musk: Reimagining the Future" or "SpaceX: Man Made Mars" offer a visual glimpse into Musk's companies, their projects, and the people who work alongside him.

Additional Resources:

- **Company Websites:** The websites of Tesla, SpaceX, Neuralink, and The Boring Company offer insights into their current projects, technological advancements, and future goals. (https://www.tesla.com/, https://www.spacex.com/, https://neuralink.com/, https://www.boringcompany.com/)
- **Articles and News Stories:** Search for online articles and

news stories featuring Elon Musk. Look for reputable publications focused on business, technology, and science to gain insights into his latest ventures, ongoing challenges, and the impact of his companies on various industries.

By exploring these resources, you can gain a richer understanding of Elon Musk's multifaceted personality. You'll delve beyond the headlines and discover the man behind the ambition, the engineer with a relentless drive to push the boundaries of what's possible.

Chapter 2: Defending the Planet and its People

Champions for a Just and Sustainable World

The 21st century isn't just about scientific breakthroughs and technological marvels. It's also a time of growing awareness about the environmental and social challenges facing our planet. In response, a new generation of heroes has emerged – **champions for a more just and sustainable world**. These passionate individuals dedicate their lives to:

◇ **Protecting the environment:** From climate change activists to conservationists, these champions fight to preserve our planet's biodiversity, reduce pollution, and promote sustainable practices. They inspire action to address issues like deforestation, ocean acidification, and the dwindling resources that sustain us.

◇ **Promoting social justice:** These champions believe in a world where everyone has the opportunity to thrive. They address issues like poverty, inequality, and discrimination. They advocate for fair labour practices, human rights, and access to education and healthcare for all.

◇ **Empowering communities:** True change requires collective action. These champions empower local communities to become stewards of their environment and advocates for their own well-being. They work alongside indigenous populations, marginalized groups, and those most affected by environmental degradation to create positive change.

Spotlighting Movements for Change:

The 21st century has witnessed a surge in powerful social and environmental movements working towards a more just and sustainable world. Here's a closer look at three such groups, each with distinct goals, methods, and significant impacts:

◈ **Fridays for Future (FFF):** Launched by Greta Thunberg in 2018, FFF is a global youth-led climate movement. Their goal is to hold world leaders accountable for addressing climate change by adhering to the Paris Agreement. Methods include student strikes every Friday, mobilizing millions worldwide to demand urgent action. FFF's impact has been undeniable, raising public awareness and pressuring governments to take climate change more seriously.

◈ **Black Lives Matter (BLM):** BLM is a decentralized movement advocating for racial justice and an end to police brutality against Black people. Formed in 2013, BLM rose to prominence following the killings of unarmed Black individuals by police. Their methods include peaceful protests, social media campaigns to raise awareness of racial bias, and calls for police reform. BLM's impact has been significant, sparking national conversations about race relations and prompting some cities to reform their police departments.

◈ **Indigenous Rights Movements:** Indigenous communities around the world are fighting to protect their ancestral lands, cultures, and self-determination. Their goals include securing land rights, preserving cultural heritage, and achieving environmental sustainability. Methods used vary depending on the specific cause, but often include protests, legal action, and community organizing. The impact of these movements is multifaceted. They have led to the return of stolen lands, recognition of Indigenous knowledge in environmental protection, and a growing global awareness of the importance of respecting Indigenous rights.

These are just a few examples. Numerous other social and environmental movements are working to create positive change in areas like gender equality, LGBTQ+ rights, and economic justice. Each movement plays a crucial role in holding powerful institutions accountable and advocating for a more just and sustainable world.

A Spectrum of Action: Diverse Approaches to Activism

The fight for a just and sustainable world is multifaceted, requiring a multitude of approaches. Activism isn't a singular path, but a spectrum of action where individuals can leverage their skills and resources to create change. Here are some ways people work towards a better future:

◈ **Peaceful Protests:** This classic form of activism brings attention to an issue and rallies public support. Marches, demonstrations, and civil disobedience can be powerful tools to disrupt the status quo and force change.

◈ **Social Media Campaigns:** The digital age has empowered activists to spread awareness and mobilize support on a global scale. Social media campaigns can use hashtags, online petitions, and creative content to educate the public and put pressure on decision-makers.

◈ **Scientific Research:** Activism isn't limited to street protests. Scientists play a crucial role by providing data and evidence to support environmental and social causes. Their research can inform policy decisions, debunk misinformation, and highlight the urgency of specific issues.

◈ **Community Development Projects:** True change often starts at the ground level. Community development projects empower local residents to address their own challenges. This might involve building sustainable housing, promoting local food systems, or advocating for educational equity within a specific neighbourhood.

These are just a few examples. Activism can take many forms, from boycotts and boycotts to boycotts and works of art. The key is to find an approach that aligns with your skills, interests, and the specific cause you're passionate about.

The Road to Change: Challenges and Triumphs

The fight for justice and sustainability is an ongoing struggle. Activists face numerous challenges, including:

◈ **Resistance from Powerful Institutions:** Corporations with vested interests and governments resistant to change can be formidable opponents. Activists may face legal battles, smear campaigns, and even physical threats in their pursuit of change.

◈ **Media Bias:** Controlling the narrative is important. Powerful interests may use media outlets to downplay the urgency of certain issues or discredit activists altogether.

◇ **Public Apathy:** Maintaining public interest and outrage over time can be difficult. Activists need to find ways to keep their message fresh and engage the public in meaningful ways.

However, despite the challenges, there have also been significant triumphs:

◇ **Policy Changes:** Activism has led to the implementation of important environmental regulations, social justice reforms, and progressive legislation.

◇ **Shifting Public Opinion:** Activism can raise awareness of critical issues and shift public opinion in favor of positive change.

◇ **Empowering Communities:** Activism fosters a sense of agency and empowers communities to take charge of their own destinies.

The victories, big and small, serve as a testament to the power of activism. They inspire future generations to continue the fight for a just and sustainable world.

The 21st century has also witnessed a rise in powerful voices advocating for a more just and sustainable world. These champions fight for the preservation of our planet and the well-being of all its inhabitants.

Let's meet such inspiring figures:

Dr. Jane Goodall

A Life Devoted to Chimpanzees and Conservation

Dr. Jane Goodall's story is one of remarkable dedication, revolutionary scientific discoveries, and a lifelong passion for chimpanzees and the natural world. Here's a closer look at her inspiring journey:

Early Life and Inspiration (1934-1960):

- Born Valerie Jane Morris-Goodall in London in 1934, Jane displayed a fascination with animals from a young age.
- Reading Tarzan stories fuelled her childhood dream of living with and studying animals in Africa.
- Despite limited opportunities for women in science at the time, Jane's determination led her to travel to Africa in 1957 to work as a secretary for renowned paleoanthropologist Louis Leakey.
- Recognizing Jane's potential and passion, Leakey offered her the ground breaking opportunity to study chimpanzees in Gombe Stream National Park, Tanzania, in 1960. This defied the scientific norm of the time, as chimpanzees were not typically studied in their natural habitat.

Revolutionizing Chimpanzee Research (1960-1970s):

- Jane's approach to studying chimpanzees was revolutionary. She broke tradition by naming them instead of using numbers, allowing her to observe their individual personalities and social behaviours.
- Her ground-breaking discoveries challenged long-held beliefs about chimpanzees. She observed them using tools, making

and modifying them for specific purposes, a behavior previously thought to be unique to humans.

- Jane documented complex social behaviours, including hunting, cooperation, and even warfare among chimpanzee groups.
- Her research not only shed light on chimpanzee intelligence and behaviour but also highlighted the close evolutionary relationship between humans and our closest living relatives.

A Champion for Conservation and Animal Welfare (1970s-Present):

- Deeply affected by the threats chimpanzees faced due to habitat loss and poaching, Jane established the Jane Goodall Institute (JGI) in 1977.
- JGI works to protect chimpanzees and their habitats, conduct ongoing research, and educate the public about the importance of conservation.
- In 1991, Jane founded the Roots & Shoots program, a global youth environmental and humanitarian program empowering young people to become agents of change in their communities.
- Through her tireless advocacy and public speaking, Jane has become a global icon for animal welfare and environmental conservation.
- She continues to travel the world, advocating for sustainable practices and inspiring millions to protect chimpanzees and the natural world.

Dr. Jane Goodall's Legacy:

- Dr. Jane Goodall's pioneering research has transformed our understanding of chimpanzees and their place in the animal kingdom.
- Her dedication to conservation and advocacy has inspired generations of scientists, activists, and everyday people to protect the environment and its inhabitants.
- Jane Goodall's story serves as a powerful reminder that one person, armed with passion and determination, can make a significant impact on the world.

Delving Deeper into the World of Dr. Jane Goodall

Dr. Jane Goodall's lifelong dedication to chimpanzees and conservation has left a profound mark on the world. Here are some resources to explore her work and achievements further:

Videos:

- **National Geographic: Jane** (Documentary film): A captivating documentary chronicling Jane Goodall's early years in Gombe and her pioneering discoveries about chimpanzees.
- **TED Talk: Jane Goodall - What separates us from chimpanzees?** (TED Talk): Dr. Goodall herself delivers a powerful talk on the intelligence and emotional lives of chimpanzees.
- **Jane Goodall Institute YouTube Channel:** https://www.youtube.com/user/JaneGoodallInstitute - The JGI channel offers a wealth of videos featuring Jane, chimpanzee behaviour, conservation efforts, and educational content.

Books:

- **In the Shadow of Man** by Jane Goodall: A classic work detailing Jane's early observations of chimpanzees in Gombe, revolutionizing our understanding of their behavior.
- **Reason for Hope: A New Kind of Animal Rights** by Jane Goodall: Explores ethical considerations of animal welfare and the importance of compassion towards all living beings.
- **Seeds of Hope: A Memoir of the Green Years** by Jane

Goodall: A personal account of Jane's early life, her passion for animals, and the founding of the Jane Goodall Institute.

Websites:

- **The Jane Goodall Institute:** https://janegoodall.org/ - The official website of the JGI provides detailed information about Jane's work, ongoing research projects, conservation efforts, and educational programs.
- **National Geographic Jane Goodall Page:** https://education.nationalgeographic.org/resource/jane-goodall/ - Offers a comprehensive overview of Jane's life, achievements, and contributions to science and conservation.

Additional Resources:

- **Roots & Shoots:** https://rootsandshoots.org/ - Explore the JGI's global youth program empowering young people to make a positive impact on their communities and the environment.
- **Jane Goodall on Social Media:** Follow Dr. Goodall on social media platforms like Twitter and Instagram (@JaneGoodallInst) for updates on her work and conservation efforts.

These resources provide a springboard for your further exploration of Dr. Jane Goodall's remarkable journey. Dive deeper into specific aspects of her work, such as her research methodologies or the challenges faced by chimpanzees in the wild. As you learn more about Jane Goodall, you'll be inspired by her unwavering dedication, scientific curiosity, and lifelong commitment to protecting our closest animal relatives and the planet we share.

Erin Brockovich

From Single Mom to Environmental Champion

Erin Brockovich's story is one of resilience, determination, and a fight for justice against seemingly insurmountable odds. Here's a glimpse into her remarkable journey:

Early Life and Challenges (1960-1992):

- Born Erin Pattee in Kansas in 1960, Erin's early life was marked by challenges. After a series of relocations and personal struggles, she became a single mother of two young children.
- Despite lacking a formal legal education, Erin possessed a strong work ethic and a fierce spirit. She pursued various careers, including waitressing and working in real estate.

A Turning Point and Uncovering the Truth (1992-1993):

- In 1992, a serious accident left Erin with injuries and financial hardship. She hired attorney Ed Masry to represent her case. While working at his law firm as a legal clerk, Erin stumbled upon a box of medical records from Hinkley, a small California town.
- The medical records revealed an unusually high number of residents suffering from illnesses like cancer and birth defects. Erin's tenacity and natural curiosity led her to investigate further.
- Through meticulous research and interviews with residents, Erin discovered a potential link between these illnesses and contaminated groundwater caused by a nearby Pacific Gas and Electric (PG&E) compressor station.

Taking on a Corporate Giant (1993-2000):

- Erin's findings became the foundation for a landmark lawsuit against PG&E. Despite scepticism from some within the firm, Erin's unwavering belief in the case and the plight of the Hinkley residents convinced Masry to take it on.
- The case hinged on proving PG&E's knowledge of the contamination and their failure to warn residents about the health risks associated with the chromium-6 tainted water.
- Erin's relentless pursuit of evidence, combined with her ability to connect with the Hinkley residents, became instrumental in building a strong case.
- After years of legal battles, a historic settlement of $333 million was reached in 1996 – the largest direct action lawsuit in U.S. history at the time.

A Voice for Environmental Justice (2000-Present):

- Erin Brockovich's story gained national attention after the release of the 2000 film "Erin Brockovich," starring Julia Roberts. The film propelled Erin into the spotlight and gave a voice to the fight for environmental justice.
- Since then, Erin has become a leading advocate for environmental awareness and consumer protection. She has used her platform to expose other cases of corporate negligence and environmental contamination, often representing communities facing similar struggles.
- She established Brockovich Research & Consulting, specializing in environmental and consumer protection issues.
- Erin is also actively involved in raising public awareness about the dangers of toxic chemicals and advocating for stricter regulations to protect public health and the environment.

Erin Brockovich's Legacy:

- Erin Brockovich's story exemplifies the power of an individual determined to fight for what is right.
- Her relentless pursuit of justice for the residents of Hinkley and her ongoing advocacy for environmental protection have inspired countless others to speak up against corporate wrongdoing.
- Erin's legacy serves as a reminder that even without a formal legal background, one can make a significant impact by combining passion, determination, and a willingness to challenge the status quo.

Delving Deeper into Erin Brockovich's Fight for Environmental Justice

Erin Brockovich's journey from a single mom to a champion for environmental justice is an inspiring story. Here are some resources to explore her life and work further:

Videos:

- **Erin Brockovich** (2000 film): This biographical drama starring Julia Roberts offers a dramatized account of Erin's work on the Hinkley case. While some liberties are taken for cinematic effect, it provides a compelling introduction to her story.

- **Erin Brockovich: A Year in the Life** (Documentary): This documentary provides a closer look at Erin's life following the Hinkley case, showcasing her ongoing work on environmental issues and her commitment to helping communities facing similar struggles.

- **Erin Brockovich Talks** (YouTube searches): You can find various interviews and talks featuring Erin Brockovich herself, where she discusses her experiences, environmental advocacy, and her perspective on corporate accountability.

Books:

- **Erin Brockovich: A Life in Love and Law** by Erin Brockovich with Beth Macy: Erin's autobiography offers a first-hand account of her life before and after Hinkley, detailing her personal struggles, challenges, and unwavering determination.

- **Take It From Here: How to Fight for What's Right and

Win by Erin Brockovich: This book serves as a call to action, sharing Erin's strategies and experiences to empower readers to take on injustice in their own communities.

- **Exposure: The Toxic Legacy of Chromium** by David Mark Feinberg: While not solely focused on Erin Brockovich, this book delves deeper into the scientific and legal aspects of the Hinkley case, exploring the dangers of chromium-6 and its impact on public health.

Websites:

- **Erin Brockovich Official Website:** https://www.brockovich.com/ - Offers information about Erin's work, ongoing environmental cases, and resources for community advocacy.
- **A Look Back: The Erin Brockovich Case** (Environmental Protection Agency website): https://www.ewg.org/news-insights/news-release/2022/10/epa-draft-review-finds-erin-brockovich-chemical-likely - Provides a summary of the Hinkley case from the EPA's perspective, highlighting the significance of the lawsuit in environmental regulations.

Additional Resources:

- **Environmental Working Group:** https://www.ewg.org/ - A nonprofit organization dedicated to protecting human health and the environment, working on issues similar to those Erin Brockovich champions.
- **Public Employees for Environmental Responsibility (PEER):** https://peer.org/ - An advocacy group that investigates environmental abuses and promotes government accountability, aligning with Erin's fight for environmental justice.

By exploring these resources, you can gain a deeper understanding of Erin Brockovich's impact, the ongoing challenges of environmental contamination, and the importance of advocating for public health and the environment. Her story serves as a powerful reminder that individuals can make a difference, inspiring future generations to fight for a cleaner and safer world.

Greta Thunberg

A Voice for Our Planet

Greta Thunberg, a young Swedish climate activist, has become a global symbol for environmental action. This chapter delves deeper into her remarkable story, exploring her early experiences, the birth of her climate activism, and the global movement she has inspired.

A Spark Ignited: Witnessing the Climate Crisis First-hand

Born in Stockholm, Sweden in 2003, Greta Thunberg's concern for the environment blossomed at a young age. At just eight years old, she learned about the devastating effects of climate change and was deeply affected by the urgency of the crisis. Unlike many adults who might compartmentalize such information, Greta's young mind couldn't ignore the impending threat. She became determined to understand the science behind climate change and the potential consequences for her generation and future generations.

From Personal Change to Collective Action

Greta's early activism began with personal efforts to reduce her own carbon footprint. She convinced her family to adopt a vegan lifestyle, reduced their air travel, and became more mindful of their energy consumption. However, she soon realized that individual actions, while important, wouldn't be enough to address the systemic issues driving the climate crisis. At the age of 11, she began researching climate activism and became inspired by the work of environmental campaigners like Winona LaDuke.

The Birth of "Skolstrejk för klimatet" (School Strike for Climate): A Solitary Stand that Sparked a Movement

In August 2018, at the age of 15, Greta decided to take a bold step. Inspired by the student walkouts for gun control happening in the United States, she decided to stage a school strike for climate outside the Swedish Parliament. Armed with a hand-painted sign that read "Skolstrejk för klimatet" (School Strike for Climate), she sat outside the parliament building every day during school hours, demanding more decisive action from the government to combat climate change.

A Message Heard Around the World: From Local Activism to a Global Movement

Greta's solitary protest quickly gained media attention. Her unwavering determination, coupled with her articulate and passionate message, resonated with people worldwide. Social media became a powerful tool, amplifying her voice and inspiring others to join her cause. Students around the globe began organizing their own climate strikes, replicating Greta's model under the banner of "Fridays for Future." Within months, a global movement had been born, uniting millions of young people in a collective demand for climate action.

Beyond Fridays for Future: Challenging World Leaders and Holding Them Accountable

Greta's activism extends beyond school strikes and social media campaigns. She has addressed world leaders at high-profile events like the United Nations Climate Action Summit, delivering powerful speeches that hold them accountable for inaction. Her unwavering stance and sharp criticism have resonated with a generation deeply concerned about the future of their planet. She has faced online trolls and media scrutiny, but her voice has only grown louder, her message reaching a wider audience with each passing day.

A Force of Nature: Greta Thunberg's Impact and Legacy

Greta Thunberg's influence on the global conversation about climate change is undeniable. She has shifted the narrative, placing the issue at the forefront of public discourse and pressuring governments and corporations to take concrete action. More importantly, she has empowered a generation of young people to become active participants in the fight against climate change.

Looking Ahead: Inspiration for a Sustainable Future

Greta Thunberg's story is one of courage, conviction, and the power of a single voice to ignite a global movement. She serves as an inspiration for young people everywhere, demonstrating the impact that individuals can have when they stand up for what they believe in. Her unwavering determination and powerful message offer a beacon of hope in the face of the climate crisis, reminding us that positive change is possible when we work together.

Further Exploration: Delving Deeper into the World of Greta Thunberg

Videos

- Watch Greta Thunberg's speech at the UN Climate Action Summit: https://www.youtube.com/watch?v=KAJsdgTPJpU

Learn more about Fridays for Future: https://fridaysforfuture.org/

◈ "https://www.youtube.com/watch?v=KAJsdgTPJpU" - This YouTube search will return various videos about Greta Thunberg, including speeches, interviews, and documentaries.

◈ "https://www.nationalgeographic.com/environment/article/greta-thunberg-reflects-on-living-through-multiple-crises-post-truth-society" - This National Geographic documentary follows Greta Thunberg for a year as she travels the world to raise awareness about climate change.

Books

◈ **No One is Too Small to Make a Difference by Greta Thunberg:** This book is a collection of Greta's speeches, essays, and scientific reports on climate change.

◈ **Our House Is on Fire: Scenes of a Planet in Crisis by Greta Thunberg:** This book features writing by Greta Thunberg alongside contributions from other climate activists.

Other Resources

◈ "https://fridaysforfuture.org/" - The website of the Fridays for Future movement, co-founded by Greta Thunberg.

◈ "https://time.com/person-of-the-year-2019-greta-thunberg/" - A Time Magazine article profiling Greta Thunberg.

◈ "https://www.britannica.com/explore/savingearth/greta-thunberg" - A biography of Greta Thunberg on Britannica.

These are just a few starting points for your exploration. There are many other resources available online and in libraries that can provide you with more information about Greta Thunberg and her activism.

- Watch Greta Thunberg's speech at the UN Climate Action Summit: https://www.youtube.com/watch?v=KAJsdgTPJpU
- Learn more about Fridays for Future: https://fridaysforfuture.org/

This chapter provides a richer understanding of Greta Thunberg's motivations, the experiences that ignited her activism, and the global movement she has inspired.

Malala Yousafzai
Champion for Education Equality

Malala Yousafzai's story is one of courage, resilience, and unwavering determination to fight for education, particularly for girls. Born in Pakistan's Swat Valley, a region heavily influenced by the Taliban, Malala defied the oppressive regime by advocating for girls' right to education. At the young age of 11, she began blogging about her experiences under Taliban rule and her desire for education. Her activism caught the world's attention, making her a target for the Taliban. In 2012, Malala was shot by the Taliban for her views, but miraculously survived.

Malala Yousafzai, a fearless advocate for girls' education and the youngest Nobel Peace Prize laureate, was born in Mingora, Pakistan in 1997. Even at a young age, Malala defied cultural norms by attending her father's private school, Khushal Girls High School. Her unwavering belief in the power of education, particularly for girls, grew stronger as the Taliban's oppressive regime took hold in her region. Despite threats and violence, Malala continued to speak out for girls' right to education, a cause that would ultimately lead to a brutal attack and propel her onto the world stage.

Instead of being silenced, Malala's voice grew even stronger. She became a global symbol for girls' education, advocating for access to education for all children, particularly girls in developing countries. Malala co-founded the Malala Fund, a non-profit organization dedicated to breaking down barriers to girls' education around the world.

Malala's story embodies the power of education to empower individuals and transform societies. She is a testament to the human spirit's ability to overcome adversity and fight for what is right. Malala Yousafzai stands as a beacon of hope, inspiring millions of girls to pursue their education and become agents of change in their communities.

Malala Yousafzai: Champion for Education Equality

Malala Yousafzai is a name synonymous with the fight for girls' education. This fearless advocate, the youngest Nobel Peace Prize laureate ever, has inspired millions with her unwavering commitment to ensuring every child, regardless of gender, has the right to an education. This expanded chapter delves deeper into her remarkable journey, the challenges she faced, and the global movement she ignited.

A Life Shaped by Education and Activism

Born in Mingora, Pakistan in 1997, Malala's life was deeply influenced by her father, Ziauddin Yousafzai, a strong proponent of education, especially for girls. He defied cultural norms by opening a school, Khushal Girls High School, where Malala received her primary education. Witnessing her father's dedication to education and the transformative power it held for girls in her community instilled a deep passion for learning within Malala from a young age.

The Taliban's Rise and the Threat to Education

However, Malala's idyllic childhood was disrupted by the rise of the Taliban in Pakistan's Swat Valley in the mid-2000s. The Taliban's extremist ideology opposed female education, and they enforced harsh restrictions, closing down girls' schools and limiting women's freedoms. Malala, however, refused to be silenced. At the tender age of 11, she began speaking out for girls' right to education, appearing on national television and writing a blog for BBC Urdu under a pseudonym. Her courage and unwavering voice made her a target for the Taliban.

A Brutal Attack and an Unwavering Spirit

In 2012, on her way home from school, Malala was shot by a Taliban gunman. The attack, intended to silence her forever, backfired spectacularly. Malala's story captured global headlines, sparking outrage and igniting a worldwide movement in support of girls' education. While the attack left her severely injured, Malala's spirit remained unbroken. After receiving medical treatment in the UK, she continued her education and activism with renewed vigour.

The Malala Fund: Empowering Girls through Education

In 2012, Malala co-founded the Malala Fund with her father. This non-profit organization advocates for girls' education globally, working to ensure every girl has access to 12 years of free, quality education. The Malala Fund invests in local education initiatives, empowers girls' rights activists, and lobbies governments to prioritize girls' education in their policies.

A Voice for Change: From the UN to Oxford

Malala's powerful advocacy transcends borders. She has addressed the United Nations, advocating for global investment in girls' education. Her inspiring speeches and unwavering commitment have made her a role model for young girls worldwide. In 2014, at the age of 17, she became the youngest Nobel Peace Prize laureate, recognized for her "struggle against the suppression of children and young people and for the right of all children to education." Malala continued her education at Oxford University, graduating in 2020 with a degree in Philosophy, Politics, and Economics, further demonstrating her dedication to learning and leadership.

Beyond Education: A Champion for Women's Rights

Malala's advocacy extends beyond education. She recognizes that education is a key component of gender equality and women's empowerment. She speaks out for girls' rights to marry when they choose, to pursue careers, and to have a voice in their communities. Her fight for education is a fight for a more just and equitable world for all girls and women.

A Legacy of Inspiration: Malala Yousafzai's Enduring Impact

Malala Yousafzai's story is one of courage, resilience, and the transformative power of education. She has become a global icon for girls' education, inspiring millions of girls to pursue their dreams and fight for their right to learn. Her unwavering commitment to education and her fight for gender equality continue to empower girls worldwide. Malala serves as a beacon of hope, reminding us that even the most vulnerable voices can ignite positive change.

Further Exploration:

Videos:

- Watch Malala Yousafzai's speech at the United Nations
- Learn more about the Malala Fund: https://malala.org[1]

◇ **He Named Me Malala (documentary):** This Oscar-nominated documentary chronicles Malala's life story, the attack by the Taliban, and her journey to becoming a global advocate for education.

◇ **Malala Yousafzai at the UN (speech):** You can find videos of Malala's powerful speeches at the United Nations on YouTube.

◇ **Malala Fund YouTube Channel:** The Malala Fund, a non-profit organization co-founded by Malala, has a YouTube channel featuring videos about Malala, education advocacy, and stories of girls' education around the world.

Books:

◇ **I Am Malala: The Girl Who Stood Up for Education and Was Shot by the Taliban by Malala Yousafzai:** This autobiography, co-written with Christina Lamb, details Malala's life story, her fight for education, and the aftermath of the Taliban attack.

---

1. https://malala.org/

◇ **We Are Displaced: My Journey and Stories from Refugee Girls Around the World by Malala Yousafzai:** This book sheds light on the global refugee crisis through Malala's perspective and the stories of other refugee girls.

◇ **Malala's Magic Pencil by Malala Yousafzai:** Aimed at younger audiences, this picture book tells a fictional story about the power of education and using your voice.

Other Resources:

◇ **Malala Fund Website:** https://malala.org/ - The Malala Fund website provides information about Malala's story, their work promoting girls' education globally, and ways to get involved.

◇ **Nobel Peace Prize Website:** https://www.nobelprize.org/uploads/2018/06/yousafzai-lecture_en.pdf - The Nobel Peace Prize website includes information about Malala's accomplishments and her Nobel Peace Prize win, along with her acceptance speech.

◇ **Malala Yousafzai on Twitter:** https://twitter.com/malala?lang=en - You can follow Malala on Twitter to get updates on her work and advocacy efforts.

David Attenborough
A Lifelong Champion for Nature

Sir David Attenborough is a name synonymous with nature documentaries and environmental advocacy. Born in the United

Kingdom in 1926, his fascination with the natural world began at a young age. This passion led him to a remarkable career at the BBC, where he produced ground-breaking natural history programs like "Life on Earth" and "Planet Earth." These captivating documentaries have brought the wonders of the natural world into living rooms across the globe, fostering a deeper appreciation for the delicate balance of our ecosystems.

Born in the United Kingdom in 1926, David Attenborough's passion for the natural world blossomed at a young age. He spent countless hours exploring the outdoors, igniting a curiosity that would shape his remarkable career. After studying zoology at the University of Leicester, Attenborough joined the BBC, where his captivating voice and unwavering enthusiasm for nature documentaries would captivate audiences worldwide.

Attenborough's impact extends far beyond entertainment. He has become a powerful voice for environmental protection, highlighting the threats posed by climate change, pollution, and habitat loss. His documentaries often serve as stark wake-up calls, prompting viewers to question their impact on the environment and inspiring action towards conservation efforts.

Throughout his long career, Attenborough has witnessed the devastating effects of human activity on our planet. However, he remains an optimist, believing that humanity can change course and ensure a sustainable future for generations to come. His tireless advocacy and unwavering commitment to environmental education make him a true champion for our planet.

David Attenborough: A Champion for Nature

Sir David Attenborough is a name synonymous with nature documentaries. His captivating voice and unwavering passion for the natural world have captivated audiences for over six decades. This expanded chapter delves deeper into his remarkable career, exploring the experiences that shaped him into a lifelong champion for nature and the impact his work has had on global conservation efforts.

A Childhood Immersed in the Natural World

Born in Leicester, England in 1926, David Attenborough's fascination with the natural world blossomed at a young age. He spent countless hours exploring the outdoors near his home, collecting fossils, and meticulously observing the wildlife around him. This early connection with nature instilled in him a deep respect for all living things and ignited a curiosity that would fuel his lifelong pursuit of knowledge.

From Studying Zoology to the BBC: A Blossoming Career

Attenborough's passion for nature led him to pursue a degree in zoology at the University of Leicester. After graduating, his exceptional communication skills and scientific background landed him a coveted position as a producer with the BBC in 1950. The BBC's nascent natural history unit provided him with the perfect platform to share his passion for the natural world with a wider audience.

Pioneering Documentary Filmmaking: Bringing Nature into Living Rooms

Attenborough's early work with the BBC involved creating educational programs about animals and their habitats. However, he recognized the need for more engaging and visually stunning documentaries that could capture the imagination of a broader audience. He pioneered innovative filming techniques, venturing deep into remote wilderness areas and utilizing cutting-edge technology to showcase the wonders of the natural world in a way never seen before.

Landmark Series: Educating and Inspiring Millions

Throughout his career, Attenborough has narrated and produced numerous landmark natural history series, each one a testament to his dedication and ground-breaking approach. Series like "Life on Earth"

(1979), "The Blue Planet" (2001), and "Planet Earth" (2006) revolutionized nature documentaries, showcasing the incredible diversity of life on Earth and the delicate balance of ecosystems.

These series captivated audiences worldwide, raising awareness about environmental issues and inspiring a generation of conservationists.

A Voice for Conservation: From Silent Witness to Vocal Advocate

While Attenborough's earlier documentaries focused on showcasing the beauty and wonder of nature, his perspective shifted over time. Witnessing the devastating effects of climate change, habitat loss, and human encroachment on wildlife, he became a vocal advocate for conservation. Documentaries like "Climate Change" (2006) and "Our Planet" (2019) delivered a powerful message about the urgency of environmental action. Attenborough's documentaries continue to be a powerful tool for raising awareness and inspiring action to protect our planet.

Beyond the Screen: A Legacy of Inspiration

Sir David Attenborough's impact extends far beyond the television screen. He has authored numerous books on natural history, narrated countless documentaries, and actively participates in conservation efforts. His unwavering dedication to nature has earned him numerous accolades, including the Order of the British Empire and the Knight Commander of the Order of the British Empire (KBE) for his services to nature broadcasting.

A Beacon of Hope for Our Planet

Sir David Attenborough's lifelong commitment to nature serves as an inspiration for generations. His work has not only entertained and educated millions, but it has also ignited a global conversation about the importance of conservation. As we face unprecedented environmental challenges, Attenborough's message of hope and his call to action serve as a powerful reminder of our responsibility to protect the planet for future generations.

Delving Deeper into David Attenborough's Life:

Sir David Attenborough is a legend in the world of natural history filmmaking. Here are some resources to explore his life, work, and the incredible natural world he's documented:

Videos about David Attenborough:

- **David Attenborough: A Life on Our Planet (documentary):** This documentary offers a glimpse into Attenborough's life, career, and his dedication to documenting the natural world.
- **David Attenborough - Little People, Big Dreams (YouTube):** This animated video, geared towards children, presents a heart-warming introduction to David Attenborough's life and achievements.

Books by David Attenborough:

- **Life on Our Planet:** A combination of stunning photography and Attenborough's characteristic narration, this book details the impact of humanity on the planet and offers a call to action for sustainable living.
- **A Life on Our Planet: My Witness Statement and a Vision for the Future:** This companion book to the documentary of the same name expands on Attenborough's observations and scientific knowledge about the environment.
- **A Life on Earth:** This classic book, published alongside the documentary series of the same name, explores the diversity of life on Earth across different habitats and ecosystems.

Documentaries by David Attenborough:

- **Life:** This ambitious series takes viewers on a journey across all corners of the globe, showcasing the incredible biodiversity of life on Earth.
- **Planet Earth:** This cutting-edge series showcases the diverse ecosystems and the challenges faced by various species across the planet.
- **The Blue Planet:** This series dives deep into the underwater world, exploring the oceans and the creatures that call them home.

Other Resources:

- **The David Attenborough Official Website:**
  https://www.youtube.com/hashtag/davidattenborough -
  This website provides information about Attenborough's
  career, upcoming projects, and conservation efforts.
- **The BBC Natural History Unit:**
  https://productions.bbcstudios.com/our-production-
  brands/the-natural-history-unit - The BBC Natural History
  Unit is the team behind many of Attenborough's
  documentaries. Their website offers behind-the-scenes
  insights and educational resources.
- **David Attenborough on Instagram:**
  https://www.instagram.com/davidattenborough/ - Follow
  David Attenborough on Instagram for breath-taking photos
  and glimpses into the natural world.

By exploring these resources, you can gain a deeper appreciation for
David Attenborough's dedication to documenting the natural world
and his lifelong passion for conservation.

Wangari Maathai
The Green Belt Movement and Planting Hope for Africa

Wangari Maathai, a Kenyan environmental activist and Nobel Peace Prize laureate, dedicated her life to restoring Africa's degraded landscapes and empowering women. Born in rural Kenya, she witnessed first-hand the devastating effects of deforestation on her community. In 1977, she founded the Green Belt Movement, a grassroots organization that mobilized women to plant trees across Africa. This simple act of planting trees brought about profound changes. It not only helped restore degraded ecosystems and combat soil erosion but also empowered women, provided them with a source of income, and fostered a sense of community ownership over environmental protection.

Wangari Maathai, a visionary environmental activist and the first woman from East and Central Africa to hold a cabinet position, was born in Ihithe, Kenya in 1940. Witnessing the devastating effects of deforestation on her community first hand, Maathai studied biology at Mount Saint Scholastic College in the United States and later received a Ph.D. in veterinary anatomy from the University of Nairobi. Upon returning to Kenya, she became deeply concerned about environmental degradation and the crucial role of women in conservation efforts.

Mathai's unwavering dedication to environmentalism faced significant opposition from the Kenyan government. Despite threats and intimidation, she continued her advocacy, eventually becoming the first woman in East and Central Africa to hold a cabinet position as Minister for Environment and Natural Resources.

Wangari Mathai's legacy extends far beyond planting trees. She demonstrated the power of community action and the crucial role women play in environmental protection. Her story is a testament to the enduring human spirit and the ability to create positive change, even in the face of adversity.

Wangari Maathai: Planting Trees, Planting Hope

Wangari Maathai, the first woman from East and Central Africa to earn a doctorate degree and the first environmentalist to win the Nobel Peace Prize, was a visionary leader who revolutionized environmental conservation in Africa. This expanded chapter delves deeper into her remarkable story, exploring her dedication to empowering women, her fight against deforestation, and the enduring legacy of the Green Belt Movement.

A Childhood Rooted in Nature and Tradition

Born in Ihithe, Kenya in 1940, Wangari Maathai's early life instilled in her a deep appreciation for the natural world and the traditional values of her Kikuyu tribe. She spent her childhood surrounded by lush forests, learning from her mother about the importance of trees and their role in maintaining ecological balance. Witnessing the changing landscape, with deforestation increasing and fertile lands becoming barren, sparked a concern for the environment that would shape her future endeavours.

Education and a Calling to Serve

Maathai's intelligence and determination led her to pursue higher education, defying societal norms that often limited girls' educational opportunities. She earned a bachelor's degree in biological sciences from the prestigious Loreto College Muñoz in Nairobi and later went on to become the first woman in East and Central Africa to receive a doctorate degree, earning a Ph.D. in veterinary anatomy from the University of Nairobi. Upon returning to Kenya, she became a professor at the university, inspiring generations of young women to pursue scientific careers.

From Scientific Research to Environmental Activism

While her scientific background provided a strong foundation, Maathai's passion for environmental issues grew. She witnessed the devastating consequences of deforestation first hand – declining water tables, soil erosion, and dwindling agricultural productivity. These challenges disproportionately impacted rural women, who relied on the land for their livelihoods. In the mid-1970s, Maathai decided to take action, founding the Green Belt Movement, a grassroots organization that would become a powerful force for environmental change.

The Green Belt Movement: Planting Seeds of Hope

The Green Belt Movement's core mission was simple yet profound – to combat deforestation and environmental degradation by planting trees. However, the initiative went beyond just planting trees. Maathai recognized the critical link between environmental health and women's empowerment. The Green Belt Movement recruited and trained women, providing them with a source of income and fostering a sense of ownership over the environmental restoration efforts. Planting trees became a symbol of hope for a better future, not just for the environment but also for the women who participated in the movement.

Facing Obstacles and Achieving Recognition

The Green Belt Movement's work was not without challenges. Maathai faced opposition from corrupt politicians who benefited from deforestation and a patriarchal society that viewed her activism with skepticism. However, her unwavering determination and powerful voice garnered international attention. The Green Belt Movement's success in planting millions of trees across Kenya and inspiring similar initiatives in other African countries led to Maathai receiving the prestigious Nobel Peace Prize in 2004. She was recognized not just for her environmental work but also for her contribution to peace and conflict resolution, demonstrating the interconnectedness of environmental health, human well-being, and social stability.

A Legacy that Continues to Grow: Beyond Planting Trees

Wangari Maathai's legacy extends far beyond planting trees. She served as an inspiration for a generation of environmental activists worldwide. The Green Belt Movement continues to thrive, empowering women and restoring degraded landscapes across Africa. Maathai's unwavering belief in the power of individuals to create positive change continues to resonate with people around the globe.

Delving Deeper into Wangari Maathai - The Woman Who Planted Trees

Wangari Maathai's legacy extends far beyond planting trees. Here are some resources to explore her life, environmental activism, and the Green Belt Movement she founded:

Books by or about Wangari Maathai:

- **Unbowed: One Woman's Fight for the Land and the Future by Wangari Maathai:** Maathai's autobiography details her journey from scientist to activist, the struggles she faced, and the triumphs of the Green Belt Movement.
- **The Green Belt Movement: Sharing the Lessons Learned by Wangari Maathai:** This book dives deeper into the philosophy and practical aspects of the Green Belt Movement, offering insights for anyone working on environmental restoration projects.
- **Planting the Trees of Peace: A Story of Wangari Maathai by Claire A. Nivola (Children's Book):** A beautifully illustrated children's book that introduces young readers to Wangari Maathai and the Green Belt Movement.

Documentaries about Wangari Maathai:

- **Wangari Maathai: The Woman Who Planted Millions of Trees:** This short documentary by PBS chronicles Maathai's life, activism, and the impact of the Green Belt Movement.
- **Taking Root: The Vision of Wangari Maathai:** This documentary explores Maathai's personal story, her fight for democracy, and the environmental impact of her work.

Videos

Wangari Maathai TED Talk: You can find Wangari Maathai's powerful TED Talk titled "The Humble Approach" online. In it, she speaks about the power of individual action and the importance of environmental conservation.

- **Wangari Maathai Nobel Peace Prize Acceptance Speech:** Witness Maathai's historic acceptance speech for the Nobel Peace Prize, the first woman from Africa to receive this honour.

Other Resources:

- **The Green Belt Movement Website:** http://www.greenbeltmovement.org/ - This website provides detailed information about the Green Belt Movement's mission, ongoing projects, and how to get involved.
- **The Nobel Peace Prize Website:** https://www.britannica.com/biography/Wangari-Maathai - Learn more about Maathai's accomplishments and her Nobel Peace Prize win on the Nobel Prize website, which includes information about her achievements and acceptance speech.
- **Articles and News Stories:** Search for articles and news stories about Wangari Maathai to gain additional insights into her activism and the impact of the Green Belt Movement.

By exploring these resources, you can gain a deeper appreciation for Wangari Maathai's incredible journey, her unwavering commitment to environmental protection, and the lasting impact of her work.

Yvon Chouinard

Patagonia's Reluctant Hero and Environmental Activist

Yvon Chouinard, the founder of Patagonia, is a unique figure who has used his business to promote environmental activism and social responsibility. Here's why he is a strong fit for this chapter:

Patagonia is not a country, it's a clothing company. It's a common misconception. Patagonia is an American outdoor apparel retailer specializing in high-quality performance clothing and gear for rock climbing, mountaineering, hiking, skiing, surfing and other outdoor activities. They are also known for their focus on environmental activism and social responsibility.

- **Environmental Advocacy:** Chouinard is a passionate advocate for environmental protection. Patagonia actively supports environmental causes and donates a significant portion of its profits to grassroots organizations fighting climate change and protecting natural areas.
- **Sustainable Business Practices:** Beyond activism, Patagonia prioritizes sustainable practices throughout its operations. They use recycled materials in their products, minimize their environmental footprint, and encourage responsible consumption habits among customers.
- **Social Responsibility:** Patagonia is known for its commitment to fair labour practices and worker well-being. They source materials ethically and advocate for fair treatment of workers throughout their supply chain.
-

Yvon Chouinard: A Leader Who Redefined Business Success

Yvon Chouinard's approach to business leadership is a breath of fresh air in a world often focused solely on profit margins. Here's a deeper look at what makes him such a unique and impactful leader:

- **Values-Driven Leadership:** Chouinard doesn't see environmental and social responsibility as add-ons; they are the very core of Patagonia's mission.
- He prioritizes protecting the environment and ensuring fair labour practices, even if it means sacrificing some potential profit. This unwavering commitment to his values inspires employees and customers alike.
- **Long-Term Vision:** Chouinard takes a long-term view of success. He believes that a healthy planet and a strong social fabric are essential for Patagonia's long-term sustainability. This focus on the bigger picture sets him apart from leaders fixated on short-term gains.
- **Building a Movement:** Patagonia isn't just a company; it's a movement. Chouinard uses his business platform to raise awareness about environmental issues and advocate for change. He encourages customers to be responsible consumers and supports grassroots organizations working towards a more sustainable future.
- **Leading by Example:** Chouinard embodies the values he espouses. He's an avid outdoorsman who leads by example, demonstrating a deep connection with nature and a commitment to living a sustainable lifestyle. This authenticity resonates with Patagonia's core audience and inspires others

to live more consciously.

Impact on Patagonia and Beyond:

Chouinard's unique leadership style has had a profound impact on Patagonia and the broader business landscape:

- **Employee Engagement and Retention:** Patagonia is consistently recognized as a great place to work. Employees are passionate about the company's mission and appreciate Chouinard's commitment to social and environmental responsibility.
- **Customer Loyalty:** Patagonia enjoys a loyal customer base who share the company's values. Customers appreciate the high-quality products and are willing to pay a premium because they believe in the brand's mission.
- **Inspiring a New Generation of Businesses:** Patagonia's success has shown that businesses can be profitable while prioritizing environmental and social responsibility. This has inspired a new generation of entrepreneurs to start companies with a positive social impact.

A Model for the Future:

Yvon Chouinard's leadership offers valuable lessons for businesses in the 21st century. His focus on long-term sustainability, environmental responsibility, and social good demonstrates that businesses can be successful while making a positive impact on the world. Patagonia is a prime example of how aligning values with business strategy can lead to long-term success.

- **Green is the New Black: How Patagonia Made Sustainability a Business Advantage by Simon Sinek:** This book explores Patagonia's success story, focusing on how the company aligns its environmental and social values with its business strategy.

- **Patagonia Website and Social Media:** The Patagonia website and social media channels showcase their commitment to environmental activism, sustainable practices, and social responsibility. (https://www.patagonia.com/)

By including Yvon Chouinard, we highlight how business leaders can be powerful forces for positive change. His story demonstrates the potential for businesses to integrate environmental and social responsibility into their core mission, contributing to a more sustainable and just future.

Dive Deeper into Yvon Chouinard's World: Resources Beyond Patagonia

Yvon Chouinard's story as a climber, surfer, businessman, and environmental activist is truly inspiring. Here are some resources to explore and gain a richer understanding of his life and philosophy:

Books:

- **Green is the New Black: How Patagonia Made Sustainability a Business Advantage by Simon Sinek:** This book explores Patagonia's success story, focusing on how the company aligns its environmental and social values with its business strategy.

- **Let My People Go Surfing: The Education of a Reluctant Businessman by Yvon Chouinard:** This autobiography is essential reading. Chouinard details his journey from a young climber to a reluctant businessman, offering insights into his love for the outdoors, his climbing career, and the founding of Patagonia.

- **Simple Patagonia: The Inspiring Business Model That Makes Money and Saves the Planet by Yvon Chouinard:** This book delves deeper into Chouinard's business philosophy. He explores the importance of environmental responsibility, building a strong company culture, and prioritizing quality over profit maximization.

- **No Shortcuts to the Top: Climbing and the Values of Self-Sufficiency by Yvon Chouinard:** This book focuses on Chouinard's climbing experiences and the lessons he learned from the sport. It highlights his love for adventure, self-reliance, and the value of pushing one's limits.

Videos:

- **Yvon Chouinard: In Conversation with [Insert Speaker Name] (Search for Talks or Interviews):** Several talks and interviews feature Chouinard discussing his life, Patagonia's mission, and his views on environmentalism and business. Look for interviews with organizations like The Nature Conservancy or business publications like Forbes.

- **Patagonia: From Climbing Gear to Environmental Activism (Documentary):** This documentary explores the history of Patagonia, how it evolved from a climbing equipment company to a leader in environmental activism. It offers insights into Chouinard's leadership and the company's core values.

- **Mission Statement (Patagonia Website):** While not a video, Patagonia's mission statement on their website is a powerful testament to Chouinard's vision. It clearly outlines the company's commitment to environmental activism and social responsibility. ([invalid URL removed])

Additional Resources:

- **Patagonia Blog and Social Media:** The Patagonia blog and social media channels offer a glimpse into the company's current environmental initiatives, social responsibility efforts, and the stories of the athletes and activists they support. (https://www.patagonia.com/blog/)

Patagonia Website and Social Media: The Patagonia website and social media channels showcase their commitment to environmental activism, sustainable practices, and social responsibility. (https://www.patagonia.com/)

- **Articles and Podcasts:** Search online for articles and podcasts featuring

Yvon Chouinard or Patagonia. Look for publications focused on business, sustainability, or outdoor activities.

By exploring these resources, you can gain a deeper understanding of Yvon Chouinard's motivations, his philosophy on leadership and business, and the impact he has had on Patagonia and the broader conversation around environmental responsibility.

Chapter 3: Artistic Expression and Cultural Impact

The 21st century has witnessed a vibrant artistic landscape, where creators push boundaries and redefine the role of art in society. This chapter explores the stories of two such visionaries who use their artistic talents to ignite conversation, challenge perspectives, and leave a lasting mark on the cultural landscape.

Redefining the Role of Art in the 21st Century

The 21st century pulsates with a vibrant artistic energy. Gone are the days of rigid styles and prescribed interpretations. Today's artists are audacious, pushing boundaries and challenging the very definition of art. This chapter delves into the stories of two such **visionaries**, creators who leverage their artistic talents to:

- **Spark Conversation:** Their work doesn't just entertain; it ignites dialogue about critical issues, social injustices, and the complexities of the human experience. They use their art as a platform to raise awareness, challenge assumptions, and spark conversations that can lead to positive change.
- **Challenge Perspectives:** These artists aren't afraid to disrupt the status quo. They challenge traditional narratives, deconstruct established norms, and offer fresh perspectives on the world around us. Their art encourages viewers to think critically, question their own biases, and see the world through a new lens.
- **Leave a Lasting Mark:** The impact of their art extends beyond the gallery walls. These visionaries create work that resonates deeply with audiences, leaving a lasting impression

on the cultural landscape. Their art shapes our understanding of the world, inspires future generations, and has the potential to spark social transformation.

This chapter will showcase the journeys of two such remarkable artists. Through their stories, we'll gain insights into the diverse ways art can be used to:

- **Reflect the complexities of the modern world:** Explore how these artists grapple with contemporary issues in their work, giving voice to the experiences and challenges of our times.
- **Embrace new forms and technologies:** Discover how these visionaries utilize innovative techniques and push the boundaries of their chosen medium.
- **Connect with a global audience:** See how art transcends language and cultural barriers, fostering empathy and understanding across the world.

By exploring the lives and works of these artistic pioneers, we gain a deeper appreciation for the power of art in the 21st century. This chapter will not only celebrate artistic brilliance but also illuminate the significant role art plays in shaping our world. This chapter explores examples of the many artists using their talents to ignite change and inspire conversation in the 21st century. As you continue reading, you'll encounter other artistic visionaries whose creativity and dedication continue to shape our cultural landscape

Beyoncé Knowles-Carter
A Voice for a Generation

Beyoncé Knowles-Carter is more than just a music superstar; she is a cultural force. Born in Houston, Texas in 1981, Beyoncé's musical talent blossomed at a young age. From her early days in the girl group Destiny's Child to her meteoric rise as a solo artist, Beyoncé has consistently redefined the boundaries of pop music. Her powerful vocals, captivating stage presence, and meticulously crafted visuals have captivated audiences worldwide.

However, Beyoncé's artistry extends far beyond catchy tunes and dazzling performances. She uses her platform to champion social justice issues, particularly those affecting women and people of colour. Her music often explores themes of empowerment, self-love, and social responsibility. Beyoncé's iconic halftime performance at the 2016 Super Bowl, featuring dancers dressed in Black Panther outfits, remains a powerful statement on race and identity in America.

Beyond Music: Expanding the Artistic Canvas

While music remains her core, Beyoncé's artistic expression extends beyond the recording studio. She co-founded the clothing line Ivy Park, blurring the lines between fashion and music. Her visual albums, like "Lemonade," are cinematic masterpieces that weave together music, storytelling, and social commentary. Beyoncé's willingness to experiment and push creative boundaries has cemented her place as a true artistic visionary.

A Voice for Empowerment and Social Change

Beyoncé Knowles-Carter is more than just a pop superstar. She is a cultural icon, a businesswoman, and a powerful voice for empowerment and social change. This expanded chapter delves deeper into her remarkable journey, exploring her rise to fame, her evolution as an artist, and her use of her platform to advocate for social justice.

From Girl's Tyme to Destiny's Child: Early Steps to Stardom

Born in Houston, Texas in 1981, Beyoncé's musical talent blossomed at a young age. She began singing and performing as a child, participating in talent shows and honing her craft. At the tender age of nine, she formed the girl group Girl's Tyme, alongside her childhood friend Kelly Rowland. This group later evolved into Destiny's Child, one of the best-selling girl groups of all time. Destiny's Child achieved immense success, topping charts and winning numerous awards. However, Beyoncé also harboured aspirations for a solo career.

A Solo Star is born: Defining Herself as an Artist and Entrepreneur

In 2003, Beyoncé released her debut solo album, "Dangerously in Love." The album was a critical and commercial success, showcasing her powerful vocals, song writing skills, and undeniable stage presence. This marked the beginning of a remarkable solo career that would solidify her position as one of the biggest stars in the music industry. Throughout her career, Beyoncé has experimented with various musical styles, from R&B and pop to hip-hop and soul. She has consistently challenged expectations, pushing creative boundaries and defying genre limitations. Beyond music, Beyoncé has also established herself as a successful businesswoman. She co-founded the entertainment company Parkwood Entertainment, giving her greater control over her creative output and business ventures.

Using Her Platform for Social Change

While Beyoncé's musical achievements are undeniable, her influence extends far beyond the Billboard charts. She has become a powerful voice for social change, using her platform to advocate for issues like racial equality, feminism, and LGBTQ+ rights. Her music videos often explore themes of social justice and empowerment, sparking conversations and inspiring action. For example, the music video for "Formation" (2016) references police brutality and the Black Lives Matter movement, while "Freedom" (2014) celebrates LGBTQ+ pride. These artistic expressions challenge societal norms and empower marginalized communities.

Beyond Music: Activism and Humanitarian Efforts

Beyoncé's commitment to social change extends beyond her music. She has actively supported various charitable causes, focusing on issues like education, disaster relief, and gender equality. She co-founded the BeyGOOD Foundation, which empowers individuals and communities worldwide. In 2018, she established the Homecoming Scholars Award Program, providing scholarships to students attending Historically Black Colleges and Universities (HBCUs).

A Role Model for a Generation

Beyoncé's influence on popular culture is undeniable. She is a role model for young women, especially women of colour, demonstrating the power of hard work, talent, and self-belief. Her music inspires confidence and self-love, while her activism encourages social responsibility and a commitment to creating a more just and equitable world.

Delving Deeper into Beyoncé's World: A Queen of Music and Culture

Beyoncé is a cultural phenomenon. Here are some resources to explore her life, musical journey, and multifaceted career:

Documentaries and Films:

- **Homecoming: A Film by Beyoncé (2019):** This documentary offers a behind-the-scenes look at Beyoncé's preparation for her historic Coachella performance in 2018.
- **Life Is but a Dream (2013):** This HBO documentary provides a glimpse into Beyoncé's personal life, her rise to

fame, and her creative process.

- **Cadillac Records (2008):** While not solely focused on Beyoncé, this film features her powerful portrayal of legendary singer Etta James.

Books by and about Beyoncé:

- **Becoming by Michelle Obama (with mentions of Beyoncé's friendship with the Obamas):** This memoir by former First Lady Michelle Obama offers insights into her personal and professional relationship with Beyoncé.
- **Beyoncé's World by J. Randy Taraborrelli:** This unauthorized biography delves into Beyoncé's life and career, from her early days in Destiny's Child to her rise as a solo artist.
- **B'Day: Beyoncé by Beyoncé Knowles-Carter:** This official companion book to her album "B'Day" features photos, lyrics, and behind-the-scenes details.

Online Resources:

- **Beyoncé's Official Website:** https://www.beyonce.com/ - Stay updated on Beyoncé's latest projects, performances, and announcements.
- **The Formation World Tour (Fan-Created Website):** https://en.wikipedia.org/wiki/The_Formation_World_Tour - This fan-created website offers in-depth analysis of Beyoncé's iconic Formation World Tour, exploring themes, symbolism, and cultural impact.
- **Scholarly Articles on Beyoncé:** Search academic databases for articles exploring the cultural significance of Beyoncé's music, performances, and activism.

Additional Resources:

- **Beyoncé's Interviews:** Find interviews with Beyoncé on YouTube and various music publications. These interviews offer insights into her creative process, artistic influences, and perspectives on social issues.
- **Beyoncé's Music Videos:** Analyse the powerful visuals and symbolism present in Beyoncé's music videos to gain a deeper understanding of her artistic vision.
- **Fan Communities:** Explore online forums and social media groups dedicated to Beyoncé. Engaging with these communities can offer fresh perspectives on her work and connect you with other passionate fans.

By delving into these resources, you can gain a richer understanding of Beyoncé's multifaceted career. Explore her evolution as a musician, her powerful performances, her business ventures, and her impact on music and popular culture. You'll discover why Beyoncé is not just a talented singer but a cultural force to be reckoned with.

Hirofumi Nakamura
Vibrant Murals and Social Commentary

Hirofumi Nakamura, a contemporary Japanese artist born in 1978, uses vibrant murals and sculptures to challenge societal norms and spark conversation. Nakamura's works often depict faceless figures, their expressions ambiguous, inviting viewers to project their own interpretations. His bold colors and dynamic compositions create visually stunning works that capture the viewer's attention.

Beyond Aesthetics: A Commentary on Society

Nakamura's art goes beyond mere aesthetics. He uses his work to address social issues like isolation, consumerism, and the digital age's impact on human connection. His recurring faceless figures represent the anonymity and alienation experienced in modern society. By prompting viewers to contemplate these themes, Nakamura's art ignites conversations and encourages critical thinking about the world around us.

Global Recognition: Art that Transcends Borders

Nakamura's work has garnered international acclaim, showcased on walls and galleries worldwide. He has collaborated with renowned brands and participated in prestigious art fairs. This global reach allows his powerful message to transcend cultural boundaries and resonate with audiences across the globe.

1. Music Composition and Performance:

Hirofumi Nakamura is involved in composing music for various productions, including musicals, stage performances, and television programs.

Notable works include:

(Dublin no Kane Tsuki Kabi Ningen): He is responsible for the music in this musical.

(Mirai Shonen Conan): He performs music in this stage production.

(Come from Away): His musical performance is featured in this production.

He has also worked on NHK (Tane no Hakobune) with the music production group **tricolor**[1][2].

Other Endeavours:

Nakamura has been involved in various creative projects:

He composed music for the dance performance (Kitokitoki Toki, Tokidokibibi) by Chapariana.

He was appointed as the **Makubetsu Town Ambassador** in 2023.

His collaborative work with **tricolour** resulted in the release of the illustrated book and music project titled **NOOK** (NOOK Volume 1).

(The World Is Wrapped in Blessings) in 2022[3][4].

Personal Projects:

Nakamura's personal song titled **"Our Birth"** was released on Bandcamp. It is a private song associated with the time during childbirth surgery[5][6].

For more details and updates, you can explore his official website[7]. Hirofumi Nakamura's diverse artistic contributions continue to inspire audiences worldwide!

.

---

1.   https://hirofuminakamura.com/

2.   https://hirofuminakamura.com/

3.   https://hirofuminakamura.com/

4.   https://hirofuminakamura.com/

5.   https://hirofuminakamura.com/

6.   https://hirofuminakamura.com/discography/our-birth/

7.   https://hirofuminakamura.com/

Frida Kahlo

A Life and Art Defined by Resilience and Identity

Early Life and Defining Tragedy:

Born Magdalena Carmen Frida Kahlo Calderon in 1907 in Coyoacán, Mexico, Frida's life was marked by both resilience and physical challenges. At the age of six, she contracted polio which left her with a permanently damaged right leg. This experience not only caused chronic pain but also became a defining theme in her artwork. In 1922, at 18, she suffered a horrific bus accident that left her with multiple fractures and a broken spine. The accident would have a lasting impact on her health, forcing her to undergo numerous surgeries throughout her life.

Artistic Awakening and Self-Portrayal:

Confined to bed for long periods after the accident, Frida turned to art as a form of expression and self-exploration. She began painting self-portraits, a genre she would become synonymous with. These portraits were unflinchingly honest, depicting not just her physical appearance but also her emotional state and inner struggles. She incorporated symbolism and imagery from Mexican folk art, creating a unique and powerful visual language.

Themes and Influences:

Frida's art explored a range of powerful themes including:

- **Identity:** Her mixed heritage (German and Mexican) and her struggles with femininity and physical limitations all played a role in her exploration of self.
- **Pain and Suffering:** The physical and emotional pain she endured throughout her life is a constant presence in her

work.

- **Sexuality and Gender Roles:** She challenged traditional beauty standards and societal expectations of women through her bold and often self-assured portrayals.
- **Mexicanidad:** Frida embraced her Mexican heritage, incorporating folk art styles and symbolism into her work.

Marriage to Diego Rivera and Turbulent Relationship:

In 1929, Frida married the renowned Mexican muralist Diego Rivera. Their relationship was passionate and complex, marked by both love and infidelity. Diego's presence is often felt in her paintings, sometimes as a source of support and other times as a source of pain.

Legacy and Cultural Impact:

Despite her physical challenges, Frida Kahlo became a leading figure in Mexican art and a feminist icon. Her work continues to resonate with viewers today, inspiring strength and self-acceptance. She challenged the art world with her raw and honest portrayals of the female experience and the human condition.

Frida Kahlo's legacy extends beyond the art world. She is a symbol of resilience, female empowerment, and Mexican cultural identity. Her vibrant personality and bold artistic style continue to influence artists and popular culture on a global scale.

Further exploration

Videos:

- **Frida Kahlo (2002):** This award-winning documentary by director Julie Taymor explores Frida Kahlo's life through a blend of archival footage, dramatic re-enactments, and animated sequences. [Available on various streaming platforms]
- **Frida Kahlo: Pain and Passion (2019):** This documentary delves into the personal struggles and artistic triumphs that

shaped Frida Kahlo's life and legacy. [Available on various streaming platforms]

- **In Her Own Words (2009):** This documentary explores Frida Kahlo's life and work through her own words and writings, narrated by actress Salma Hayek. [Available on various streaming platforms]

Additional Reading Resources:

- **"The Diary of Frida Kahlo: An Intimate Self-Portrait" by Frida Kahlo:** This beautifully illustrated book features excerpts from Frida Kahlo's personal diary, offering a glimpse into her thoughts, feelings, and creative process.
- **"Frida Kahlo" by Hayden Herrera:** This comprehensive biography is considered a classic on Frida Kahlo's life and work. It delves into her artistic development, personal relationships, and the cultural context that shaped her art.
- **"Looking at Frida Kahlo" by Andrea Kettenmann:** This book provides a critical analysis of Frida Kahlo's paintings, exploring the symbolism, influences, and feminist themes present in her work.

These resources offer a deeper dive into Frida Kahlo's life, artistic journey, and lasting impact. Happy exploring!

Ai Weiwei

A Rebellious Artist Shaping China's Narrative

Ai Weiwei, born in 1957 in Beijing, China, is more than just an artist; he's a cultural force, a relentless activist, and a thorn in the side of the Chinese government. His life and work are a powerful testament to the fight for creative freedom and social justice.

Early Life and Artistic Awakening:

The son of a prominent poet ostracized by the Communist regime, Ai's childhood was marked by political exile and the harsh realities of censorship. This instilled in him a rebellious spirit and a deep curiosity for the world outside China. In 1981, he ventured to the United States, immersing himself in the vibrant art scene of New York City. Here, he discovered the works of Marcel Duchamp and Andy Warhol, artists who challenged traditional notions of art. This exposure would significantly influence his own artistic development.

Returning to China and Championing the Avant-Garde:

After a decade abroad, Ai returned to China in 1993. He found himself amidst a burgeoning avant-garde art movement pushing boundaries and critiquing social norms. He co-founded the China Art Archives & Warehouse (CAAW), a vital platform for independent artists and a space fostering open dialogue. Ai's own work began to gain recognition. He utilized unconventional materials like wood, metal, and even recycled objects to create sculptures and installations that were both visually arresting and politically charged.

Social Activism and Clash with Authority:

Ai Weiwei's art transcended aesthetics. He became a vocal critic of the Chinese government's human rights record, its suppression of free speech, and its handling of environmental issues. He utilized social media to expose government corruption and advocate for transparency.

One of his most well-known acts of defiance involved collecting the names of children killed in the devastating 2008 Sichuan earthquake due to poorly constructed schools. This investigation exposed government negligence and sparked public outrage.

Detention, Exile, and Continued Influence:

In 2011, Ai Weiwei was detained by Chinese authorities for 81 days. The charges were vague, but it was widely seen as retaliation for his activism. Despite constant surveillance and limitations on his movement within China, Ai continued his fight for creative freedom. He used his international platform to raise awareness about human rights abuses in China and inspire others to challenge authority. In 2015, he finally left China and has since established himself as a global voice for dissent.

A Legacy of Challenging the Status Quo:

Ai Weiwei's influence extends far beyond the art world. He is a symbol of resistance, a champion for free speech, and a relentless advocate for social justice. His work continues to spark conversations about censorship, government accountability, and the power of individual expression. Ai Weiwei has redefined the role of the artist in the 21st century, proving that art can be a powerful tool for social change.

Further exploration

Videos:

◇ **Ai Weiwei: Never Sorry (2012):** This award-winning documentary offers an intimate look at Ai Weiwei's life, his artistic process, and his clashes with the Chinese government. [Available on various streaming platforms]

◇ **Ai Weiwei: Yours Truly (2018):** This documentary explores Ai Weiwei's global influence and his ongoing fight for freedom of expression. [Available on various streaming platforms]

◇ **#AiWeiwei (2018):** This TED Talk by Ai Weiwei himself delves into his creative vision and his belief in the artist's responsibility to challenge authority. TEDTalks YouTube Channel

Additional Reading Resources:
"Weiwei: Writings on Art and Dissent" by Ai Weiwei: A collection of Ai Weiwei's writings, interviews, and essays that provide insight into his artistic philosophy and his views on social and political issues.

"Ai Weiwei: Sunflower Seeds" by Sunflower Seeds Exhibition Catalog: This catalogue offers a detailed look at Ai Weiwei's iconic "Sunflower Seeds" installation, exploring its artistic and social significance.

"Ai Weiwei: Rupture" by Robin Pogrebin and Li Zhang: A comprehensive biography that delves into Ai Weiwei's personal life, artistic development, and his ongoing struggle for creative freedom in China.

Nina Simone

From Child Prodigy to Civil Rights Icon

Born Eunice Kathleen Waymon in 1933, Nina Simone's life story is a testament to artistic brilliance, resilience in the face of racism, and the power of music as a tool for social change.

A Musical Prodigy:

Music surrounded Nina from a young age. By the age of three, she was already playing piano by ear, and by six, she was performing at church services. Her talent was undeniable, and with the help of her community, she was sent to study classical piano at prestigious institutions like Julliard.

Dreams Deferred:

Simone's dream was to become a concert pianist, the first African American classical pianist on the world stage. However, her aspirations were met with a harsh reality. Despite a successful audition, she was denied admission to the Curtis Institute of Music in Philadelphia. While the reasons remain unclear, Simone believed it was due to racial prejudice.

Birth of Nina Simone:

Unable to pursue her classical dreams, Simone reinvented herself. She began performing at nightclubs under the stage name Nina Simone, adopting a more commercial sound that incorporated jazz, blues, and folk. Her powerful vocals, infused with raw emotion, captivated audiences. Hits like "I Loves You, Porgy" established her as a rising star.

A Voice for the Civil Rights Movement:

The 1960s saw a shift in Simone's music. The escalating racial tensions in America deeply affected her. Songs like "Mississippi Goddam" and "To Be Young, Gifted and Black" became anthems for the Civil Rights Movement. Her concerts transformed into powerful declarations of social justice, her voice a weapon against oppression.

Beyond Music:

Simone's activism extended beyond music. She befriended prominent figures like Martin Luther King Jr. and Malcolm X, and participated in rallies and protests. She also used her platform to speak out against the Vietnam War and advocate for equality. Here's an expanded look at Nina Simone's activism beyond music:

Beyond Melody: A Life Woven with Activism

Nina Simone's commitment to social justice wasn't just expressed through her music; it was a deeply ingrained part of her life. Here's a closer look at her activism:

- **Friendship with Civil Rights Leaders:** Simone's talent and social awareness attracted prominent figures in the Civil Rights Movement. She befriended Martin Luther King Jr. and shared his dream of racial equality through nonviolent resistance. However, after the assassination of Medgar Evers and the Birmingham church bombing, her frustration with the slow pace of change resonated more with the more militant stance of Malcolm X.

- **From Stage to Streets:** Simone wasn't content with just singing about injustice. She actively participated in rallies and protests, lending her voice and influence to the movement. She performed benefit concerts to raise funds for civil rights organizations, using her platform to raise awareness and inspire action.

- **Anti-War Activism:** The Vietnam War was another target of Simone's activism. Songs like "Why? (The King of

Mississippi)" and "To Hell with War" expressed her fierce opposition to the conflict. She saw it as a continuation of the oppression faced by Black Americans at home.

- **A Global Voice for Equality:** Simone's struggles against racism extended beyond the American context. She embraced her Pan-African identity and spoke out against colonialism and oppression worldwide. Songs like "Backlash Blues" and "Young, Gifted and Black" became anthems for Black liberation movements across the globe.

Impact and Legacy:

Nina Simone's activism wasn't without personal consequences. Her outspoken nature led to clashes with some within the Civil Rights Movement and the music industry. Yet, her courage and unwavering commitment to justice left a lasting impact. She inspired a generation of artists and activists to use their voices to fight for a more equitable world.

A Life of Complexity:

Simone's life wasn't without its struggles. Personal difficulties and mental health issues plagued her later years. Disillusioned with the ongoing racial struggles in America, she eventually left the US and resided in various countries throughout Europe and Africa.

A Legacy of Inspiration:

Despite her challenges, Nina Simone's legacy remains unmatched. She was a ground-breaking artist who defied categorization, a powerful voice for the voiceless, and a testament to the enduring power of music to inspire change. Her music continues to be celebrated and reinterpreted by new generations, a lasting reminder of her artistry and unwavering commitment to social justice.

Delving deeper into Nina Simone's life.

We can explore a wealth of resources that bring her story and music to life.

Video Resources:

- **What Happened, Miss Simone? (2016):** This award-winning documentary by Liz Garbus offers a comprehensive look at Simone's life and career, including her rise to fame, her activism, and her personal struggles.
- **Nina Simone: Live at Montreux 1976 (1976):** This concert film captures Simone's electrifying live performance, showcasing her powerful vocals and stage presence.
- **Nina: A Story of Nina Simone (Narrated Read Aloud):** This beautifully illustrated children's book, narrated on YouTube, offers a heart-warming introduction to Simone's life and music.

Book Recommendations:

- **I Put a Spell on You: The Autobiography of Nina Simone (1991):** Co-written with Stephen Cleary, this autobiography provides a first-hand account of Simone's life, from her childhood experiences to her rise to fame and beyond.
- **Nina Simone: Break Down and Let it all Out (2004):** Written by Sylvia Hampton and David Nathan, this biography delves into Simone's complex personality and the challenges she faced throughout her life.
- **Princess Noire: The Tumultuous Reign of Nina Simone (2010):** Nadine Cohodas' biography explores Simone's life through a feminist lens, examining her struggles as a Black woman in the music industry.

Chimamanda Ngozi Adichie
The Power of Storytelling and Reclaiming Narratives

Chimamanda Ngozi Adichie is a world-renowned novelist, nonfiction writer, and public speaker whose work explores themes of identity, race, gender, and colonialism. By including Chimamanda Ngozi Adichie, we add a diverse voice to this chapter. Her work highlights the power of storytelling in challenging stereotypes, promoting understanding, and giving voice to the marginalized.

- **Storytelling and Social Commentary:** Adichie's powerful storytelling tackles complex social issues. Her novels, like "Americanah" and "Half of a Yellow Sun," explore the experiences of immigrants, the legacy of colonialism, and the complexities of race and identity.
- **Giving Voice to the Marginalized:** Adichie's work amplifies the voices of those often overlooked or marginalized. Her characters challenge stereotypes and offer nuanced perspectives on contemporary issues.
- **Cultural Impact:** Adichie's writing has had a global impact. Her novels are translated into numerous languages, and she's a prominent voice in discussions on race, gender, and post colonialism.
- **The Power of Language:** Adichie emphasizes the importance of language in shaping narratives. Her TED Talk, "The Danger of a Single Story," highlights the dangers of stereotypes and the need for diverse narratives.

Chimamanda Ngozi Adichie: A Powerful Voice for Our Times

Amplifying Marginalized Voices:

Chimamanda Ngozi Adichie's literary works consistently elevate the experiences of those often excluded from mainstream narratives. Here's a deeper look at how she achieves this:

- **Characters Who Challenge Stereotypes:** Adichie's novels don't rely on simplistic portrayals. Her characters, like the Nigerian immigrants in "Americanah" or the characters caught in the Biafran War in "Half of a Yellow Sun," are complex individuals grappling with identity, belonging, and the challenges of navigating a world shaped by race, gender, and colonial legacies.
- **Nuance over Monolith:** Adichie avoids portraying Africa or any other culture as a monolith. Her stories showcase the rich diversity within cultures and challenge simplistic generalizations.
- **Giving Voice to the Unheard:** Through her characters, Adichie sheds light on experiences often overlooked in mainstream literature. She explores the struggles of immigrants, the impact of colonialism, and the complexities of navigating cultural expectations and personal desires.

Global Impact and Cultural Influence:

Adichie's work transcends geographical boundaries and resonates with readers worldwide. Here's how her writing has had a global impact:

- **International Recognition:** Adichie's novels are translated into numerous languages, making her work accessible to a vast global audience. She has received prestigious literary awards, solidifying her place as a major voice in contemporary literature.

- **Sparking Conversations:** Adichie's writing tackles critical issues around race, gender, and post colonialism. Her work sparks conversations and challenges readers to examine their own biases and perspectives.
- **A Shift in Narratives:** Adichie's success contributes to a broader shift in the literary landscape. Her work encourages a more inclusive and diverse range of stories to be told and heard, enriching the global literary conversation.

The Power of Language and Storytelling:
Chimamanda Ngozi Adichie is a strong advocate for the power of language and storytelling in shaping our understanding of the world. Here's why this is a central theme in her work:

- **The Danger of a Single Story:** In her renowned TED Talk, "The Danger of a Single Story," Adichie warns against relying on one-dimensional narratives. She emphasizes the importance of seeking out diverse perspectives and understanding the limitations of a single story in capturing the complexities of human experience.
- **Language and Identity:** Adichie explores the intricate connection between language and identity. Her characters often navigate the complexities of speaking and writing in multiple languages, reflecting the realities of a globalized world and the impact of colonialism on language and cultural expression.
- **The Power of Literature:** Adichie believes that literature has the power to break down barriers, foster empathy, and challenge the status quo. Her writing aims to create a more

informed and compassionate world through the power of storytelling.

By elaborating on these aspects, we paint a more comprehensive picture of Chimamanda Ngozi Adichie's impact. She is not just a talented writer; she's a powerful voice who uses her platform to challenge stereotypes, amplify marginalized voices, and promote a more just and equitable world through the power of language and storytelling.

Dive Deeper into Chimamanda Ngozi Adichie's World: Exploring Her Life and Work

Chimamanda Ngozi Adichie's journey as a writer and cultural icon is as captivating as her novels. Here are some resources to delve deeper into her life story and the themes explored in her work:

Books by Chimamanda Ngozi Adichie:

- **Start with her novels:**
    - **Americanah:** Explores the experiences of Nigerian immigrants navigating love, identity, and race in the United States.
    - **Half of a Yellow Sun:** A powerful story set against the backdrop of the Biafran War in Nigeria, showcasing the human cost of conflict.
    - **Purple Hibiscus:** A coming-of-age story that tackles themes of family, religion, and personal freedom.
- **We Should All Be Feminists:** This powerful essay, also available as a short audiobook, explores the importance of feminism for men and women alike.
- **Dear Ijeawele, or A Feminist Manifesto in Fifteen Suggestions:** A collection of advice written to a new mother, offering insight into raising a feminist daughter.

Videos and Online Talks:

- **TED Talk: The Danger of a Single Story:**
  (https://www.ted.com/talks/
  chimamanda_ngozi_adichie_the_danger_of_a_single_story?lang
  This must-watch TED Talk explores the power of storytelling
  and the dangers of relying on simplistic narratives.
- **Interviews and Discussions:** Search online for interviews
  featuring Adichie discussing her writing process, her views on
  contemporary issues, and the role of literature in society.
  Look for platforms like BBC News, The New Yorker, or
  literary festivals like PEN World Voices.

Documentaries and Films:

- **Half of a Yellow Sun (2013 Film):** Based on Adichie's novel, this film
  offers a visual portrayal of the Nigerian Civil War and its impact on
  individuals and families.

Additional Resources:

- **Chimamanda Ngozi Adichie's Website:** While not overly
  extensive, her website offers biographical information,
  upcoming events, and links to her published works.
  (https://www.chimamanda.com/)
- **Literary Criticism and Articles:** Numerous articles and
  scholarly works analyze Adichie's writing style, themes
  explored in her novels, and her impact on contemporary
  literature. Search online databases or academic journals for
  in-depth analyses.

By exploring these resources, you can gain a richer understanding
of Chimamanda Ngozi Adichie's life, her influences, and the driving

force behind her powerful storytelling. Her voice continues to challenge stereotypes, spark conversations, and inspire readers worldwide.

Chapter 4: Innovation and Entrepreneurship

Igniting Change in the 21st Century

The 21st century has witnessed an explosion of creativity and ingenuity, ushering in a new era of innovation and entrepreneurship. This chapter delves into the captivating stories of individuals who dared to dream beyond the ordinary. These visionary entrepreneurs not only challenged the status quo but also ignited change across various sectors, shaping the world we live in today.

A Landscape of Opportunity:

Several factors have fuelled this surge in innovation. The rapid advancement of technology has opened doors for innovative ideas and disruptive businesses. Globalization has fostered a more connected world, facilitating the exchange of ideas and talent. A growing emphasis on social impact has driven entrepreneurs to address pressing global challenges.

Meet the Change makers: Within this dynamic landscape, we encounter a diverse range of entrepreneurs. Some, like Elon Musk, have revolutionized entire industries with their audacious ventures in aerospace and electric vehicles. Others, like Reshma Saujani, have championed social change through initiatives like Girls Who Code, promoting equal opportunities in the tech sector. As you delve deeper into the chapters, you will discover the fascinating stories of these individuals. We will explore their journeys, from the spark of inspiration to the challenges they faced in turning their ideas into reality. We will learn about the innovative solutions they developed and the impact they have had on the world.

Beyond Inspiration:

This chapter is not merely a collection of inspiring stories. It aims to equip you with valuable insights into the world of entrepreneurship. By analysing the approaches of these successful individuals, you may discover principles and strategies relevant to your own aspirations. Perhaps you harbour the seeds of a ground-breaking idea or a burning desire to create positive change. The stories in this chapter can serve as a source of inspiration and practical knowledge, empowering you to embark on your own entrepreneurial journey.

Sir Richard Branson

A Virgin Voyage through Innovation and Entrepreneurship

Sir Richard Branson's story is a testament to the power of audacious dreams, relentless determination, and a healthy dose of rebellion. He embodies the spirit of innovation and entrepreneurship, defying expectations and carving a unique path through the business world.

Early Life and a Rebellious Spirit (1950-1970):

- Born in 1950, Richard Branson displayed an entrepreneurial streak from a young age, selling parakeets and Christmas trees as a teenager to raise funds for his first magazine, Student.
- Diagnosed with dyslexia, Richard struggled in traditional schooling but possessed an infectious curiosity and a knack for creative problem-solving.

Virgin Records: Birth of a Brand (1970-1980s):

- In 1970, Richard's entrepreneurial spirit blossomed with the launch of Virgin Mail Order Records, a mail-order record business catering to a growing demand for affordable music.
- He opened the first Virgin Records store in 1972, offering a wider selection and a more welcoming atmosphere than traditional record shops. Virgin Records quickly gained a reputation for supporting up-and-coming artists, signing iconic acts like the Sex Pistols and The Rolling Stones.
- Richard's innovative approach extended beyond music. He challenged industry norms by launching Megastores, offering a one-stop shop for music, movies, and books.

Beyond Records: Building a Virgin Empire (1980s-Present):

- Branson's entrepreneurial spirit didn't stop at music. In 1984, he defied established airlines by launching Virgin Atlantic, offering a more customer-centric flying experience.
- Virgin Group, the umbrella corporation encompassing all his ventures, continued to expand, venturing into travel, mobile communications, financial services, and even space tourism with Virgin Galactic.
- Throughout his ventures, Richard embraced innovation and a sense of adventure. He challenged the status quo, offering alternative choices to consumers and disrupting established industries.

More than Business: A Legacy of Adventure and Philanthropy:

- Richard Branson is not just a businessman; he is a renowned adventurer. He has broken numerous records in hot air ballooning and transatlantic crossings, demonstrating his thirst for exploration and pushing boundaries.
- He is also a dedicated philanthropist, using his resources to champion environmental causes and support social entrepreneurship initiatives.

Richard Branson's Enduring Influence:

- Sir Richard Branson's story serves as an inspiration for aspiring entrepreneurs. He exemplifies the importance of following one's passion, embracing innovation, and challenging the status quo.
- His success story, however, is not without its complexities. Some criticism surrounds the financial practices of Virgin businesses.

- Despite such complexities, Richard Branson's legacy is undeniable. He has built a vast and diverse empire, challenged established industries, and instilled a spirit of adventure and risk-taking in the world of business.

Delving Deeper into Richard Branson's Daring Adventures & Business Acumen

Sir Richard Branson's life is a whirlwind of audacious ventures, entrepreneurial triumphs, and a constant push for innovation. Here are some resources to explore his story further:

Videos:

- **Branson: Balancing Business and Adventure** (Documentary): This documentary offers a glimpse into Branson's life, balancing his business ventures with his adventurous spirit.
- **Richard Branson Interviews:** Search YouTube for various interviews where Richard Branson discusses his career path, business philosophies, and perspectives on entrepreneurship.
- **Virgin TED Talks:** Several TED Talks feature Richard Branson himself or Virgin Group representatives. These talks delve into topics like innovation, disruption, and the importance of customer experience.

Books:

- **Losing My Virginity** by Richard Branson: Branson's autobiography, offering a firsthand account of his early ventures, building the Virgin brand, and his experiences in the business world.
- **Screw It, Let's Do It: Richard Branson's Story** by Richard Branson: Another autobiographical work by Branson,

focusing on his approach to business, his entrepreneurial spirit, and his philosophy of embracing challenges.

- **The Virgin Way: If It's Not Fun, It's Not Business** by Richard Branson with Patrick Wright: Branson outlines his business principles, emphasizing fun, a customer-centric approach, and a culture of empowerment within Virgin companies.

Websites:

- **Virgin Group Website:** https://www.virgin.com/about-virgin/virgin-group: The official Virgin Group website provides information about all Virgin companies, Branson's ventures, and his philanthropic initiatives.
- **Richard Branson Blog:** https://www.virgin.com/branson-family/richard-branson-blog: Branson shares his thoughts on business, adventure, and current issues on his personal blog.
- **Forbes Profile - Richard Branson:** https://www.forbes.com/profile/richard-branson/ - This Forbes profile offers a concise overview of Branson's career, business achievements, and net worth.

Additional Resources:

- **Follow Richard Branson on Social Media:** Stay updated on Branson's latest ventures and initiatives by following him on platforms like Twitter (@richardbranson) and Instagram (@richardbranson).
- **Read Articles on Virgin Companies:** News outlets regularly cover Virgin's various ventures. Explore online articles to gain insights into specific businesses and how they continue to disrupt their industries.

By delving into these resources, you can gain a deeper understanding of Richard Branson's multifaceted personality, his innovative business strategies, and the impact he has had on the world of entrepreneurship. His story serves as an inspiration to take risks, challenge the norm, and build a business empire fueled by passion and a commitment to a unique customer experience.

By including Sir Richard Branson in our chapter on Innovation and Entrepreneurship, we showcase a different kind of entrepreneur. His story emphasizes the importance of defying expectations, taking calculated risks, and building a brand that reflects a specific vision and customer experience.

Reshma Saujani

Championing Girls in Tech

Reshma Saujani is a lawyer, politician, and the founder of Girls Who Code, a non-profit organization dedicated to closing the gender gap in the tech industry. Her journey embodies innovation, social impact, and a relentless pursuit of creating equal opportunities for girls in the field of technology.

Early Life and Education (1975-Present):

- Born in Illinois in 1975, Reshma is the daughter of Indian immigrants who fled Uganda due to political unrest. Raised with a strong work ethic and a focus on education, Reshma excelled in school and developed a passion for social justice.
- She graduated with degrees in Political Science and Speech Communication from the University of Illinois Urbana-Champaign. Later, she earned a Master's degree in Public Policy from Harvard University's John F. Kennedy School of Government and a Juris Doctor from Yale Law School.

From Law and Politics to Tech Advocacy (1990s-2010):

- Reshma began her career as an attorney and Democratic organizer, working on social justice issues. In 2009, she made history as the first Indian-American woman to run for Congress, representing New York's 14th congressional district.
- During her campaign, Reshma visited local schools and witnessed the stark underrepresentation of girls in computer science classes. This experience became a turning point in her career.

Building Girls Who Code (2010-Present):

- Inspired by the need to empower girls in technology, Reshma founded Girls Who Code in 2010. The organization offers after-school programs, summer camps, and online resources that teach girls coding skills, build their confidence, and introduce them to the exciting possibilities of tech careers.
- Under Reshma's leadership, Girls Who Code has grown exponentially. It serves girls in all 50 states and has impacted the lives of hundreds of thousands of young women.
- Reshma is also a bestselling author, with books like "Brave, Not Perfect" encouraging girls to overcome self-doubt and embrace their potential.
- **Reshma Saujani's Legacy:**

- Reshma Saujani's innovative approach to closing the gender gap in tech has garnered international recognition.
- Her work with Girls Who Code has inspired countless young women to pursue careers in computer science, opening doors to exciting opportunities in a rapidly evolving field.
- Reshma's legacy extends beyond technology. She advocates for a future where girls and women hold leadership positions across all sectors, fostering a more diverse and equitable society.

By highlighting Reshma Saujani's story, we can showcase the power of social entrepreneurship and the importance of advocating for equal opportunities in the tech industry. Her work serves as an inspiration to all who believe in the potential of girls and young women to shape the future of technology.

Deepening Your Dive into Reshma Saujani's

Work with Girls Who Code

Reshma Saujani's dedication to empowering girls in technology is an inspiring story. Here are some resources to delve deeper into her work and the impact of Girls Who Code:

Videos:

- **TED Talk: Reshma Saujani - Teach girls bravery, not perfection** (TED Talk): https://www.youtube.com/watch?v=ltoLOeE7K4A - Reshma delivers a powerful TED Talk discussing the importance of teaching girls bravery and confidence to bridge the gender gap in tech.
- **Girls Who Code - Our Story** (YouTube video): https://www.youtube.com/user/girlswhocode - This video provides an overview of Girls Who Code's mission, programs, and the impact it has on young girls interested in technology.
- **Girls Who Code Interviews** (YouTube searches): Several interviews with Reshma Saujani can be found online, offering insights into her background, motivations, and vision for Girls Who Code.

Books:

- **Brave, Not Perfect: Girls Who Code on Friendship, Family, and Finding Your Voice** by Reshma Saujani: Aimed at young women, this book encourages them to embrace challenges, overcome self-doubt, and pursue their dreams.
- **Girls Who Code: Closing the Gender Gap in Technology** by Reshma Saujani: This book delves deeper into the gender gap in tech and Girls Who Code's approach to bridging this gap by equipping girls with the necessary skills and

confidence.

- **Lean In: Women, Work, and the Will to Lead** by Sheryl Sandberg: While not solely focused on Reshma or Girls Who Code, this book by Facebook COO Sheryl Sandberg explores gender equality in the workplace and offers valuable insights for women pursuing careers in tech.

Websites:

- **Girls Who Code:** https://hq.girlswhocode.com/ - The official Girls Who Code website offers comprehensive information about their programs, resources, and the impact they create.
- **Reshma Saujani's Website:** https://reshmasaujani.com/girls-who-code/ - Provides information about Reshma's career journey, Girls Who Code, and her advocacy for girls in technology.
- **National Centre for Women & Information Technology (NCWIT):** https://ncwit.org/resource/bythenumbers/ - A non-profit focused on increasing the participation of women and girls in computing and technology.

Additional Resources:

- **Follow Girls Who Code and Reshma Saujani on Social Media:** Stay updated on their latest initiatives and connect with a community passionate about girls in tech by following them on platforms like Twitter, Instagram, and Facebook.
- **Explore Girls Who Code Alumni Stories:** The Girls Who Code website features stories of young women who have participated in their programs and are now pursuing careers in technology. These stories offer inspiring examples of the

impact Girls Who Code has on its participants.

By exploring these resources, you'll gain a deeper understanding of Reshma Saujani's vision, Girls Who Code's innovative approach, and the lasting impact they have on girls interested in the ever-evolving world of technology.

Blake Mycoskie
TOMS Shoes and the One-for-One Movement

Blake Mycoskie, born in Waco, Texas in 1972, isn't your typical entrepreneur. Driven by a desire to make a positive impact, his innovative business model has transformed the shoe industry and redefined the concept of social responsibility. During a trip to Argentina, Mycoskie witnessed the hardships faced by children lacking proper footwear. This experience sparked an idea: a for-profit business model that could provide shoes to those in need.

Thus, TOMS Shoes was born. For every pair of TOMS purchased, a new pair of shoes would be donated to a child in need. This "one-for-one" model resonated with consumers, turning TOMS into a global phenomenon. TOMS has since expanded its giving program to include eyewear, providing sight-saving treatments and glasses.

Beyond Shoes: A Movement for Social Good

Blake Mycoskie's vision with TOMS wasn't just about distributing shoes, it sparked a revolution in how businesses approached social responsibility. Here's a deeper look at the "one-for-one" movement and its lasting impact:

The Rise of "One-for-One" Businesses:

- **A New Business Model:** TOMS' "one-for-one" model, where a product purchased triggers the donation of a similar item to someone in need, became a blueprint for a new wave of socially conscious businesses. Companies across various industries began adopting similar models, integrating social good into their core operations.
- **Examples of Inspiration:** Warby Parker, the eyewear

company, followed suit with their "Buy a Pair, Give a Pair" program, providing glasses to those in need. Brands like Patagonia, focusing on environmental sustainability, and FEED, donating meals with every product purchase, are just a few examples of companies inspired by TOMS.

- **A Shift in Consumer Consciousness:** TOMS' success highlighted a growing consumer demand for companies to be socially responsible. Customers became more interested in brands that aligned with their values, creating a market for businesses that did good while doing well.

Impact of the Movement:

- **Increased Social Impact:** The "one-for-one" model led to a significant increase in resources directed towards social causes. Companies donating a portion of their profits or products translated to real-world improvements in areas like healthcare, education, and environmental protection.
- **Empowering Consumers:** The movement empowered consumers to make a difference through their purchasing decisions. They could actively support causes they cared about simply by buying products they already wanted.
- **Challenges and Criticisms:** The "one-for-one" model also faced some criticism. Some argued it might be a form of "slacktivism," a feel-good approach that didn't address the root causes of social problems. Others questioned the long-term sustainability of some models and the effectiveness of the donated products or services.

TOMS' Legacy:

- **A Pioneering Force:** Despite the critiques, TOMS' role in igniting the "one-for-one" movement remains undeniable. They played a pivotal role in changing the conversation around corporate social responsibility and pushing businesses to consider their social impact.

- **Evolving Model:** TOMS itself has also evolved its model beyond shoes. They now address issues like access to clean water and sight. This adaptability demonstrates a commitment to finding effective ways to create positive change.

The "one-for-one" movement may not be a perfect solution, but it undoubtedly spurred a significant shift in the business landscape. By making social good an essential part of their strategy, companies are not only responding to consumer demands but also contributing to a more positive and sustainable future.

Delving Deeper into Blake Mycoskie's World: Resources Beyond Shoes

Blake Mycoskie's journey with TOMS is an inspiring story of entrepreneurial spirit and social impact. To delve deeper, here are some resources to explore:

Videos:

- **TOMS Founder Blake Mycoskie — Fear{less} with Tim Ferriss (https://www.youtube.com/@timferriss)** : This interview dives into Mycoskie's entrepreneurial journey with TOMS. Tim Ferriss, a renowned investor and author, discusses the challenges and triumphs of building a socially conscious business.

- **Blake Mycoskie on the Process of Renewal as an Enneagram 7 (S04-004) (https://m.youtube.com/watch?v=0yJFv3gnJrU)** : This video offers a glimpse into Mycoskie's personal side. He discusses his experiences through the lens of the Enneagram, a personality typing system.

- **My Conversation With the Founder of TOMS, Blake Mycoskie (https://m.youtube.com/watch?v=0yJFv3gnJrU)** : This interview focuses on the inspiration behind TOMS and the power of a simple idea to create positive change.

Books:

- **Start Something That Matters by Blake Mycoskie** : This autobiography details Mycoskie's path from a reality TV contestant to the founder of TOMS. It offers insights into his entrepreneurial mindset and the challenges of building a purpose-driven business.

- **Give and Take: Why Helping Others Drives Our Success by Adam Grant** : This book explores the concept of givers, takers, and matchers in professional settings. Mycoskie's story of building TOMS aligns with the "giver" mentality, offering valuable lessons about the power of generosity in business.

- **The Purpose Driven Life by Rick Warren**: Mycoskie has cited this book by Rick Warren as an influence on his approach to business and life. It explores the importance of finding purpose and living a life that makes a difference, a theme central to TOMS' philosophy.

Additional Resources:

- **TOMS Website:** The TOMS website provides detailed information about the company's mission, impact, and current initiatives. They also share stories of the people they serve and the positive change they create. (https://www.toms.com/)
- **Social Media:** Follow TOMS on social media platforms like Instagram, Facebook, and Twitter to stay updated on their latest projects and connect with their community. These platforms also offer glimpses into Mycoskie's ongoing involvement with the company.
- **Articles and Podcasts:** Searching online for articles and podcasts featuring Blake Mycoskie or TOMS will reveal additional insights and perspectives.

By exploring these resources, you can gain a richer understanding of Blake Mycoskie's vision, the challenges and triumphs of building TOMS, and the lasting impact of the "one-for-one" movement.

Whitney Wolfe Herd
Bumble and Empowering Women

Whitney Wolfe Herd, born in Salt Lake City, Utah in 1989, is revolutionizing the dating app landscape by empowering women. After co-founding Tinder, she left the company due to concerns about its culture and safety issues. However, Wolfe Herd didn't shy away from the challenge. Fuelled by her desire to create a more respectful and empowering dating experience for women, she launched Bumble in 2014.

Bumble: Changing the Dating Game

Bumble's unique feature is that only women can initiate conversations, breaking the traditional mould and shifting the power dynamic. This approach has resonated with millions of users seeking a more respectful and intentional dating experience. Bumble's success highlights the importance of addressing user needs and creating a platform that prioritizes safety and mutual respect.

Beyond Dating: A Broader Vision for Bumble and Whitney Wolfe Herd

Whitney Wolfe Herd's ambition for Bumble extends far beyond the realm of online dating. Here's a deeper look at how Bumble is working towards a more holistic vision:

Empowering Women beyond Dating:

- **Bumble Bizz and Bumble BFF:** The app has expanded its functionality beyond romantic connections. Bumble Bizz focuses on professional networking, while Bumble BFF helps users build platonic friendships. This creates a more comprehensive platform for women to connect and support each other in all aspects of life.

- **Partnership with Empowering Organizations**
- Bumble actively partners with NGOs and charities that champion women's causes. This includes organizations focused on women's rights, education, entrepreneurship, and safety. Some examples include Malala Fund, The Global Fund for Women, and Girls Who Code.
- **Investing in Women-Led Businesses**
- Bumble Ventures, the company's investment arm, focuses on funding businesses founded and led by women. This provides financial backing to female entrepreneurs and fosters innovation in various sectors.

Inspiring a Generation of Women Leaders - Whitney Wolfe Herd as a Role Model:

- Wolfe Herd's own story, overcoming challenges and achieving success in a male-dominated industry, serves as a powerful inspiration to young women. She embodies the power of ambition, resilience, and using one's platform to advocate for change.
- **Bumble Hive:** This online community connects Bumble users with each other and with inspiring female leaders. It provides a platform for mentorship, networking, and sharing stories that empower women to pursue their goals.

Challenges and Considerations - Balancing Social Impact with Profitability. Balancing social responsibility with financial success is a constant challenge for for-profit businesses like Bumble. Critics might argue that some initiatives are primarily marketing strategies.

- **Measuring the Impact:** Quantifying the true impact of Bumble's social efforts can be difficult. Measuring the long-term effects of partnerships, investments, and community initiatives requires ongoing evaluation.

Overall Impact:

Bumble, under Wolfe Herd's leadership, is striving to become more than just a dating app. They are working towards creating a social ecosystem that empowers women, fosters connections, and promotes positive change in the broader world. The company's efforts, while not without challenges, offer an interesting model for how businesses can integrate social responsibility into their core mission.

Delving Deeper into Whitney Wolfe Herd's World: Resources beyond Bumble

Whitney Wolfe Herd's journey as an entrepreneur and advocate for women's empowerment is an inspiring story. Here are some resources to explore and gain a richer understanding of her life and accomplishments:

Videos:

- **The Tim Ferriss Show - Whitney Wolfe Herd (https://www.youtube.com/watch?v=ca5h47tJsdE)** : This interview with Tim Ferriss, a renowned investor and author, offers insights into Wolfe Herd's entrepreneurial journey. She discusses the challenges of building Bumble, her vision for the future, and advice for aspiring entrepreneurs.
- **Whitney Wolfe Herd Explains Why Bumble Clapped Back at One User (https://www.youtube.com/watch?v=nKs9tURTAJY)** : This short video showcases Wolfe Herd's leadership style and commitment to Bumble's core principles. She addresses a situation where the company took a strong stance against inappropriate user behaviour.
- **Small changes with big impact (with Bumble's Whitney

Wolfe Herd) | Masters of Scale (https://www.youtube.com/watch?v=nKs9tURTAJY) : This episode of Masters of Scale, a show exploring successful businesses, features Wolfe Herd discussing Bumble's origins and evolution. She delves into how small tweaks can lead to significant changes in user behaviour and platform culture.

Books:

- **Lean In: Women, Work, and the Will to Lead by Sheryl Sandberg**: While not directly about Wolfe Herd, this book by Facebook COO Sheryl Sandberg explores challenges women face in the workplace and offers advice on overcoming them. Wolfe Herd has cited Sandberg as a role model and an inspiration for her own leadership style.
- **Bad Blood: Secrets and Lies in a Silicon Valley Start-up by John Carreyrou**: This investigative book details the rise and fall of Theranos, a fraudulent blood-testing company. Wolfe Herd's experience working at Theranos before founding Bumble sheds light on her early exposure to the dark side of Silicon Valley culture.
- **#Girlboss by Sophia Amoruso**: This memoir by Sophia Amoruso, founder of fashion brand Nasty Gal, chronicles her journey as a young entrepreneur. Wolfe Herd may find inspiration in Amoruso's story of building a successful business in a competitive industry.

•

Additional Resources:

- **Bumble Blog:** The Bumble blog features articles written by Wolfe Herd and other team members. These articles offer insights into the company's mission, initiatives, and perspective on women's empowerment. (https://thebeehive.bumble.com/bumbleblog)
- **Whitney Wolfe Herd on Social Media:** Follow Wolfe Herd on platforms like Instagram and Twitter to stay updated on her activities, get a glimpse into her life beyond Bumble, and see the causes she champions.

Articles and Podcasts:

Searching online for articles and podcasts featuring Whitney Wolfe Herd will reveal additional perspectives on her life, leadership style, and vision for Bumble. Look for interviews with business publications, women's empowerment organizations, and tech industry leaders.

By exploring these resources, you can gain a deeper understanding of Whitney Wolfe Herd's ambitions, the challenges she has faced, and the impact she strives to create through Bumble and her advocacy efforts.

Mukesh Ambani
Building a Digital Revolution in India

Mukesh Ambani, the chairman and managing director of Reliance Industries, is a prime example of innovation and entrepreneurship in the 21st century, particularly within the Indian context. Here's why he'd be a great fit:

- **Digital Transformation:** Reliance Jio, a subsidiary of Reliance Industries spearheaded by Ambani, revolutionized India's telecom sector by offering affordable high-speed internet access. This move brought millions online, contributing significantly to India's digital transformation.
- **Entrepreneurial Spirit:** Ambani has consistently diversified Reliance Industries beyond its traditional focus on oil and gas. He has ventured into sectors like retail, telecommunications, and digital services, demonstrating a proactive approach to identifying new opportunities.
- **Impact on the Indian Economy:** Reliance Industries is one of the largest companies in India, employing millions and contributing significantly to the country's GDP. Ambani's vision and leadership have played a crucial role in India's economic growth.
- **Global Recognition:** Ambani is a prominent figure on the global business stage. His achievements have garnered international recognition, showcasing India's entrepreneurial potential on a worldwide scale.
-

Mukesh Ambani: Global Recognition and India's Rise as a Tech Powerhouse

Beyond Prominence: Mukesh Ambani's global recognition transcends mere "prominence." Here's a deeper look at how his achievements showcase India's potential as a tech leader:

- **Rankings and Awards:** Ambani consistently ranks high on global business leader lists. His recent ranking as the second-highest scoring CEO in the Brand Guardianship Index 2024 highlights his reputation for innovation and social responsibility.

- **Investments and Partnerships:** Reliance Industries under Ambani's leadership has attracted significant foreign investment from global tech giants like Google and Facebook. These partnerships showcase India's attractiveness as a tech hub and Ambani's role in facilitating such collaboration.

- **Jio's Impact on the Global Stage:** The success of Reliance Jio has been studied and celebrated internationally as a model for affordable and accessible internet access. This has placed India at the forefront of discussions regarding digital inclusion and bridging the digital divide.

- **A Beacon for Aspiring Entrepreneurs:** Ambani's story inspires aspiring entrepreneurs worldwide, particularly in emerging economies. His success demonstrates the potential for home-grown innovation to disrupt established markets and create a global impact.

India's Rise as a Tech Leader:

Ambani's achievements are not just a personal triumph; they contribute to India's rise as a major player in the global tech landscape. Here's how his vision aligns with India's tech ambitions:

- **Digital India Initiative:** The Indian government's "Digital India" initiative aims to transform the country into a digitally empowered society. Reliance Jio's contribution to increasing internet penetration aligns perfectly with this national vision.
- **Building a Local Tech Ecosystem:** By fostering innovation within Reliance and collaborating with other Indian start-ups, Ambani is contributing to the development of a robust local tech ecosystem in India.
- **Changing the Narrative:** For decades, India's image was primarily associated with outsourcing and low-cost labour. Ambani's success helps shift the narrative, showcasing India's potential for domestic innovation and leadership in the tech sector.
-

Delving Deeper into Mukesh Ambani's World: Resources beyond Reliance

Mukesh Ambani's story is one of ambition, innovation, and shaping India's economic landscape. Here are some resources to explore and gain a richer understanding of his life and achievements:

- **Business News Articles and Interviews:** Numerous articles and interviews with Ambani offer insights into his strategies, vision, and impact on the Indian economy.
- **Reliance Industries Website and Social Media:** The Reliance Industries website and social media channels provide information about the company's diverse ventures

and Ambani's leadership approach.

- **Documentaries and Books on Indian Business Leaders:** Documentaries and books focusing on Indian business leaders might offer a broader context for understanding Ambani's place within the Indian economic landscape.

Books:

- **A Complete Biography of Mukesh Ambani by A.K. Gandhi**: This biography offers a detailed account of Ambani's life, from his early days to his rise as a business leader. It explores his strategies, challenges, and the factors that contributed to his success.

- **Persevere and Prevail Like Mukesh Ambani by Rajiv Agarwal**: This book focuses on Ambani's key decisions and leadership style. By analysing his business strategies, Agarwal provides insights into Ambani's approach to entrepreneurship and navigating the complexities of the Indian market.

- **Ambani & Sons by Hamish McDonald**: This book takes a broader view, exploring the Ambani family and their business legacy. It provides context for Mukesh Ambani's rise within the Reliance Empire and the family dynamics that have shaped the company's direction.

- **Beyond the Boardroom: Books & shows that capture Mukesh Ambani's wisdom, words and wit (The Economic Times)**: This article from The Economic Times offers a curated list of books and documentaries related to Mukesh Ambani and Reliance Industries. (https://economictimes.indiatimes.com/topic/latest-mukesh-ambani-news)

Videos:

- **Mukesh Ambani's Picks | Best Books To Read | Weekend Masti | CNBC Awaaz (https://m.youtube.com/watch?v=RczPUmnK4c8)** : This CNBC Awaaz segment features Mukesh Ambani himself. He discusses his favourite books and offers insights into his leadership philosophy and approach to business.

- **Reliance Industries Limited - Company Profile**: This corporate profile video provides a high-level overview of Reliance Industries, showcasing its diverse business ventures and achievements. While not focusing solely on Ambani, it offers a glimpse into the company he leads.

- **Documentaries on Indian Business Leaders:** Documentaries focusing on the rise of Indian business tycoons or the history of Indian business houses might offer valuable context for understanding Ambani's place within the larger economic landscape. Search online for documentaries featuring titles like "Indian Captains of Industry" or "The Rise of Indian Business."

Additional Resources:

- **Reliance Industries Website and Social Media:** The Reliance Industries website and social media channels offer information about the company's various ventures, its leadership team, and news related to Mukesh Ambani. (https://www.ril.com/)

- **News Articles and Interviews:** Numerous business news articles and interviews with Mukesh Ambani provide insights into his vision, strategies, and perspectives on the Indian economy. Search for articles from reputable publications like

The Economic Times, The Times of India, or Forbes India.

By exploring these resources, you can gain a deeper understanding of Mukesh Ambani's journey as an entrepreneur and his impact on India's economic and technological transformation.

By including Mukesh Ambani, we showcase a unique perspective in this chapter. He exemplifies innovation and entrepreneurship within an emerging economy, highlighting the impact such individuals can have on a national and even global scale.

Jacqueline Novogratz
Building Financial Inclusion through Innovation

Jacqueline Novogratz is a social entrepreneur who champions financial inclusion for the world's poorest populations. By including Jacqueline Novogratz in Chapter 4, we showcase a different kind of entrepreneur. Her focus on social impact and financial inclusion highlights the power of innovation to address global challenges and empower marginalized communities.

- **Innovative Solutions:** Novogratz founded Acumen, a non-profit organization that invests in and supports innovative financial services for the underserved. These services, like microloans and mobile banking, empower individuals to build a better future.
- **Focus on Impact:** More than just creating businesses, Novogratz emphasizes the social impact of financial inclusion. Access to financial services allows people to escape poverty, invest in their families, and build stronger communities.
- **Scaling Change:** Acumen focuses not just on individual ventures but also on scaling successful models across different regions. This ensures a broader impact and empowers more people through financial inclusion.
- **Entrepreneurial Spirit:** Novogratz embodies the entrepreneurial spirit. She identified a critical gap in financial services for the poor and developed innovative solutions to bridge that gap.
-

Jacqueline Novogratz: A Champion for

Financial Inclusion

Jacqueline Novogratz is a visionary leader who isn't just building businesses; she's building a more inclusive and equitable world through innovative financial solutions. Here's a deeper look at her work and its impact:

- **Pioneering Financial Inclusion:** Novogratz recognized a critical gap in traditional financial services - the millions of people living in poverty who lacked access to basic financial tools. Traditional banks often overlook these populations due to perceived risk.

- **Acumen: Investing in Change:** In 2001, Novogratz founded Acumen, a non-profit organization with a revolutionary approach. Instead of simply donating money, Acumen invests in and supports innovative financial service providers working with the underserved.

- **Impactful Solutions:** Acumen supports a diverse range of ventures – microfinance institutions offering small loans, mobile banking platforms reaching remote communities, and financial literacy programs empowering individuals to manage their finances effectively.

- **Beyond Transactions: Building a Better Future:** Financial inclusion isn't just about access to money. It's about empowering individuals and families to break free from poverty cycles. Access to loans allows them to start businesses, invest in education, and build a more secure future.

- **Scaling the Impact:** Novogratz and Acumen don't just support individual ventures; they focus on scaling successful models across different regions. This ensures broader impact and empowers more people around the world.

A New Model for Philanthropy:

Novogratz's approach to social change challenges traditional philanthropic models. Here's what sets her apart:

- **Investing vs. Donating:** Acumen invests in financial service providers, allowing them to become sustainable businesses. This creates a long-term impact model compared to traditional one-time donations.
- **Market-Based Solutions:** Novogratz believes in the power of the market to drive positive change. By investing in sustainable and impactful businesses, Acumen helps create an ecosystem that empowers low-income communities.
- **Focus on Sustainability:** The goal isn't just to create a temporary solution; it's to build financially self-sufficient organizations that can continue supporting low-income populations for years to come.

A Global Movement:

Novogratz's work with Acumen has inspired a global movement towards financial inclusion. Here's how her work is making a difference:

- **Empowering Millions:** Acumen has supported hundreds of financial service providers, impacting millions of people living in poverty across the globe.
- **Sparking Innovation:** Novogratz's work encourages innovation in the financial services sector, leading to new approaches that better serve underserved populations.
- **A Shift in Thinking:** Novogratz's efforts are contributing to a broader shift in how we address poverty. Financial inclusion is increasingly recognized as a critical tool for empowering individuals and fostering sustainable development.

By including Jacqueline Novogratz, we showcase an inspiring example of how innovation and entrepreneurship can be harnessed to tackle some of the world's most pressing challenges. Her work with Acumen offers a hopeful and impactful approach to building a more inclusive financial system that empowers individuals and communities worldwide.

Delving Deeper into Jacqueline Novogratz's World: Resources beyond Acumen

Jacqueline Novogratz's journey as a social entrepreneur and champion for financial inclusion is as inspiring as her work with Acumen. Here are some resources to explore and gain a richer understanding of her life, motivations, and the impact she has had:

Books by Jacqueline Novogratz:

- **Charitable Choices: The Three Forces that Drive Effective Philanthropy**: In this book, Novogratz delves into the world of philanthropy, challenging traditional models and advocating for a more strategic and impactful approach. She explores the three key forces that drive effective giving: passion, smart analysis, and perseverance.
- **Field Notes from a Philanthropist: The Power of Untapped Capital**: This book offers a first-hand account of Novogratz's experiences working with Acumen. She shares stories of the entrepreneurs and individuals impacted by Acumen's investments, highlighting the power of financial inclusion to transform lives.

Videos and Online Talks:

- **TED Talks**: Several TED Talks feature Novogratz discussing Acumen's work, financial inclusion, and the fight against poverty. Search for titles like "The Return on Compassion" or "How to Change the World with Patient Capital".

- **Interviews and Podcasts**: Look for interviews on platforms like Forbes, The World Bank, or podcasts focused on social impact or social entrepreneurship. These interviews offer insights into Novogratz's perspectives on global development, philanthropy, and the future of financial inclusion.

- **Acumen YouTube Channel**: The Acumen YouTube Channel (https://www.youtube.com/@acumenfund) features several short videos highlighting the stories of entrepreneurs and individuals impacted by Acumen's investments. These offer a glimpse into the human impact of Novogratz's work.

Additional Resources:

- **Articles and Features**: Numerous articles and features explore Novogratz's work with Acumen and the impact of financial inclusion. Search online publications focused on business, development, or social impact for in-depth analyses and perspectives.

- **Jacqueline Novogratz Website**: Novogratz's personal website (https://www.instagram.com/jnovogratz/?hl=en) offers a brief biography, information about her books, and links to some of her talks and interviews.

By exploring these resources, you can gain a deeper understanding of Jacqueline Novogratz's journey, her vision for a more inclusive financial system, and the ongoing impact of her work through Acumen.

- **Acumen Website:** The Acumen website

(https://acumen.org/) provides information about the organization's work, its investment philosophy, and the stories of people impacted by financial inclusion.

- **Talks and Interviews:** Search online for talks and interviews featuring Jacqueline Novogratz. Look for platforms like TED Talks, conferences on social entrepreneurship, or podcasts focused on social impact.

Conclusion

A World Ignited, a Future Shaped Together

As you've journeyed through the stories of these remarkable individuals, you've witnessed the power of a single spark – a spark of curiosity, a spark of compassion, a spark of innovation. These sparks have ignited movements, revolutionized industries, and redefined the very landscape of the 21st century.

But the impact doesn't stop there. Each spark has the potential to create a ripple effect, inspiring and empowering others to ignite their own flames of change. The scientist's discovery paves the way for future breakthroughs. The activist's fight for justice paves the way for a more equitable world. The artist's challenge to societal norms inspires others to express themselves authentically.

The champions you've encountered are not anomalies. They represent the boundless potential that resides within each of us. We all have the power to ignite our own sparks, to identify the areas in our world that need change and contribute our unique talents and perspectives.

This book is not just a collection of biographies; it's a call to action. It's an invitation to join a global community of change makers. Let the stories you've read inspire you to find your own cause, your own passion. Perhaps you'll become a scientist unravelling the mysteries of the human body, an activist fighting for social justice, or an artist using your creativity to challenge societal norms.

The possibilities are limitless. The world needs your spark – your unique contribution to the ever-evolving tapestry of the 21st century. But remember, you don't have to walk this path alone. Connect with others who share your passions, collaborate on projects, and amplify each other's voices. Together, our collective sparks can ignite a fire that illuminates the path towards a brighter future. Go forth, ignite your passion, and leave your mark on the world, for the impact you create will ripple outward, inspiring and empowering others to do the same.

www.ingramcontent.com/pod-product-compliance
Lightning Source LLC
Chambersburg PA
CBHW061344160726
47995CB00001B/164